You Cannot Fail!

Gods Covenant to Man

Pastor Gloria Taylor-Boyce
and
Pastor Ralph H Boyce

Copyright © 2014 Pastor Gloria Taylor-Boyce and Pastor Ralph H Boyce
All rights reserved.

ISBN: 1500844314
ISBN 13: 9781500844318
Library of Congress Control Number: 2014914821
CreateSpace Independent Publishing Platform
North Charleston, South Carolina

The Lord God hath given me the tongue of the learned, that I should know how to speak a word in season to him that is weary: he wakeneth morning by morning, he wakeneth mine ear to hear as the learned.
Isaiah 50:4

The Master, God, has given me a well-taught tongue, So I know how to encourage tired people. He wakes me up in the morning, Wakes me up, opens my ears to listen as one ready to take orders.
Isaiah 50:4, The Message Bible

This book is dedicated to all the members and friends of Zoe Ministries International, Canada; local church and conference-call partners, without whose love and constant physical, mental, and spiritual encouragement this book might never have been. We love you all

TABLE OF CONTENTS

FOREWORD	vii
CHAPTER ONE: The Fight Is Over	1
CHAPTER TWO: Abundance Is Your Inheritance	17
CHAPTER THREE: Are We Victims Of Circumstances?	27
CHAPTER FOUR: Claim Your Truth	39
CHAPTER FIVE: Why Are You Here?	55
CHAPTER SIX: What Are You Seeing?	63
CHAPTER SEVEN: We Are Always Evolving	69
CHAPTER EIGHT: The Mind Is The Battleground	77
CHAPTER NINE: How To Retain Information	85
GLOSSARY OF TERMS	95
ABOUT THE AUTHORS	103

Foreword

ALL ACTION IS the result of thought. Look around you. All that you see was once only imagined. The clothes you wear, the chair you are sitting in, all of it was once a thought. This is the law that is the everlasting standard, for all things must bring forth after their kind; in essence you can only create from your thoughts. The very first chapter of the book of Genesis states this reality:

> And God said, let the earth bring forth the living creature after his kind, cattle, and creeping thing, and beast of the earth after his kind: and it was so. And God made the beast of the earth after his kind, and cattle after their kind, and everything that creepeth upon the earth after his kind: and God saw that it was good. (Genesis 1:24–25)

This is the identical harvest, meaning that you create according to what you envision. As long as the earth endures, there will be seedtime and harvest. Your thoughts are the seeds that produce after their kind. You can only manufacture your thoughts.

The word of God is quite clear: Give, and it shall be given unto you (Luke 6:38). In this work, authors and pastors Gloria Taylor-Boyce and Ralph Boyce show you that you have been receiving what you have been requesting. The problem is that you cannot stop the blessings from coming unto you. You request it; he delivers it. However, you may not realize what you are requesting, for your heart may be saying one thing while your mouth says another.

As people of God, we are sowing and giving of ourselves daily. Once you give, a void is created, and that void becomes full again; that is one law you have no control over. If you give love you will receive love. The question is: How can you attract the right kind of blessings into your life? Or more broadly, can you even attract a certain kind of blessing in the first place? The answer is yes, and it is embedded in the contents of this work's title: *You Cannot Fail: God's Covenant to Man.*

As people of faith, we want to do what is right, and we often wonder if we are doing the Father's will. As you read this book, come with an open mind to new concepts, for obviously the old belief system is not working. I call upon you to test yourself to make sure you do not believe in two powers, for there is only one power.

> Arise, and go down to the potter's house, and there I will cause thee to hear my words. Then I went down to the potter's house, and, behold, he wrought a work on the wheels. And the vessel that he made of clay was marred in the hand of the potter: so he made it again another vessel, as seemed good to the potter to make it. Then the word of the Lord came to me, saying, O house of Israel, cannot I do with you as this potter? saith the Lord. Behold, as the clay is in the potter's hand, so are ye in mine hand, O house of Israel. (Jeremiah 18:2–6)

Enjoy the book *You Cannot Fail.* It is God's covenant to man.

1

The Fight is Over

"And he said, Let me go, for the day breaketh. And he said, I will not let thee go, except thou bless me."
(Genesis 32:26)

Mankind is fickle, and its ways are subject to change from day to day. However, God is constant. He is the same yesterday, today, and forever. As you progress through the teachings in this book, you will discover one dominant principle: It is impossible to satisfy flesh. If your goal is to please mankind, you choose to go down the road of insanity. You can please flesh for a moment, and that is it. However, when your purpose is to please and obey God, then you realize that you do what you do because it is the right thing to do. In doing this, you submit to God within you and operate in excellence. If you stay focused on the divine and your sole purpose is to please God, you will experience unspeakable joy. You will exude that essence, and your actions will please those around you. The only way to become one with your heavenly Father is to submit to God within you. So what is holding you back from progressing? The fight is over! Your only stumbling block is fear.

Fear often is the single emotion that limits many people from reaching their potential. Fear just seems to grip them, almost as if they were in a trance. This happens even though scripture tells us that God did not give us a spirit of fear but of courage and a strong mind (2 Timothy 1:7). This fear appears to be triggered by want and lack. However, many people seem to experience the fear of the unknown. This emotion hangs on in spite of what the book of Genesis tells us—that God made us in his image and likeness (Genesis 1:27). Look here! I am not just talking about high-risk takers. This passage also refers to decent, honest individuals who just want to live a pleasant life and raise their families. However, there is always a struggle.

What if I were to tell you that the fight is over? What if I were to tell you that you cannot fail? What if I were to tell you that everything comes into your life for your greater good? Today the giant in you is about to be awakened. Hear me out. When you encounter new experiences in your life, especially issues that affect your security, this can trigger survival instincts and the "flight-or-fight" stress responses. If you are not sure that you are secure in the world, the fear can become more intense.

For example, fear can intensify if you lose your job and are not sure how you will pay your bills. Even if the change is positive, such as getting married, you can still feel elements of fear because you are making a change and do not know all the possible consequences. A deeper fear that you may not be aware of is the fear of death. Every moment is unique and dies and gives birth to the next moment, but because it is predictable, people see life as continuous. However, when something more obvious ends in your life, such as a relationship, there is generally a pause before something new comes in.

Unfortunately, during this pause or void, nothing much seems to happen or move forward. It's like we are stuck on pause, unsure about what will happen next or when it will happen, and usually at this point we worry about what could go wrong and try to fill the gaps. The first question we need to ask, then, is: Why do we struggle with knowing that God made us in his image and likeness? The second question is: Can we change this pattern of thinking?

The answer is yes, you can change your pattern of thinking because change is the only constant variable. Could I also tell you that focusing on the past is the very reason your problems keep showing up in your life? Know this: You are not the source of your prosperity! You never have been. God is the ultimate source, and his grace grants you the power to order and manifest whatever kind of reality you can create. All new things begin as ideas in a fertile imagination, including inventions, governments, art, and even spiritual doctrines.

We have only to hold his marvelous concepts in our minds, and gradually, the forces of the universe pool and gather like an accumulating electrical current to break into the material plane and give us our desires. That is the nature of the manifestation of his good. However, when we think, we can multiply outside ourselves; when we think that we could create in the physical before first seeing it and developing it in our minds, we are turning our backs on that truth and betraying everything God has given us.

Prosperity Starts Within

Everything first exists in your mind before it exists in the physical world, including that feeling of lack and limitation. When times are hard, you must first look within because your own mind is shaping the world around you. Look at what Jeremiah 18:2–6 says:

> Up on your feet! Go to the potter's house. When you get there, I'll tell you what I have to say. So I went to the potter's house, and sure enough, the potter was there, working away at his wheel. Whenever the pot the potter was working on turned out badly, as sometimes happens when you are working with clay, the potter would simply start over and use the same clay to make another pot. Then God's Message came to me: Can't I do just as this potter does, people of Israel? God's Decree! Watch this potter. In the same way that this potter works his clay, I work on you, people of Israel.

Are you adhering to your core values and focusing your mind on them at all times? If you are, then you will know it because those values will manifest themselves in your life. If a woman who defines prosperity as fidelity and freedom from debt bases her entire being on those values, fidelity and financial freedom will constantly come into her orbit. She will enjoy a faithful mate, and debt will rarely stay around for long. However, if that same woman tosses away those fundamental values and lets her mind be drawn to the shallow, base pursuit of material things, she will focus on what she does not have. Then lack will infect her mind, and eventually it will become her reality.

No matter how we act, this fact does not change: the mind is always shaping the fabric of reality on the spiritual level just like the potter shapes the clay. When you narrow the power of the mind with your purpose and focus on the result, your desires will be fulfilled because that power is creative. As Isaiah 46:10 says, "Declaring the end from the beginning, and from ancient times, the things that are not yet done, saying, my counsel shall stand, and I will do all my pleasure."

However, when you let thoughts of greed, anxiety, and envy run loose, they will turn the mind's power against you. Your wayward thinking becomes a self-fulfilling prophecy. Am I suggesting that millions of people brought about their own unemployment and financial ruin? Not exactly! Some things just happen because the destructive energies set in motion by other minds years before must fulfill their purpose.

A few minds can make decisions that result in the eventual dissolution of a corporation and all its jobs. What I'm leading to is this: Because you judge others by their behavior and yourselves by your intentions, your personal intention can do little about other people's behavior. However, your mind can redirect the course of your life if you are focused on the values that make you who you are.

For example, if you worked for a company that could possibly go out of business soon and your mind was oriented only on the fear of unemployment and poverty, then you would suppress your divine ability to attract new opportunities into your orbit because you would broadcast nothing but fear and worry to the universal mind. However, if your eyes were set on an unchanging set of values (e.g., creativity, giving to others, and health), then you would manifest those things in your life and probably find new employment in a creative or nonprofit field that would not only bring you a paycheck, but also greater fulfillment.

Who Are You?

Before moving on, let us identify the truth of who you are. Many theologians and writers of spiritual works start with the Bible because it details the beginning of time. To address the question of who you are, you also should go to the first book in the Bible, the book of Genesis. A chief feature of Genesis is the acceptable way that it answers the question of mankind's origins. Genesis

1:1–2 says, "In the beginning, God created the heaven and the earth. And the earth was without form, and void." Know this: When you orient your thoughts to become the thing that you desire and never waver, you can achieve virtually anything in this world, even the supposedly impossible. The mind is your mouthpiece to God, and God sees through all fabrications. However, you must remember that even when you lie to yourself, some part of you knows it.

Even when you convince yourself that everything will be all right, you cannot deceive that celestial component of your mind. Whether or not you choose to listen often determines how your life will progress. So when you fix your attention on something that appears promising, such as complete healing, you may believe that because your mind is focused on that outcome, it will come to pass. Nevertheless, the godly mind knows that your attention is born of fear or desperation, and those are the things that you will ultimately manifest! It is impossible to entertain even the deepest self-delusion without part of the mind knowing the truth. It is better not to discover your impractical dream at all than to delude yourself into thinking it real, and to set aside all other priorities to bring it into your material reality and wreak havoc on your world. In essence, you are who you say and believe you are.

Understanding of Self
It takes courage to face the truth because the truth is not always what we would like to have. We face the steadfast challenge of having two minds: the mind that exists in linear time and sees only limitations, and the mind that is our pulsating, living connection to the Almighty, which is without time and which knows that what we see today is temporary. Our lives are an unmoving conflict between our base minds and our enlightened minds. To further understand this, let us start at the beginning. In the

beginning God created, and this marks the creation of the absolute beginning of the temporal and material world.

There can be no beginning without a word. This segment of the Bible also outlines the process of creation. As you ponder each word, you will start to see how the Bible defines your identity. First, Genesis says that in the beginning, "God created." That word *created* is significant. It denotes action and it also denotes creation, for there must be a mental action in the beginning of every creation. The word *form* also plays an important part in self-identification and purpose as outlined in the book of Genesis 1:2. "Without form" means that, in essence, there were only vastness, nothingness, and nonexistence. Come to think of it you cannot form without having first created the object in the mind.

Next we come to Genesis 1:15: "And God made the beast of the earth after his kind and cattle after their kind, and everything that creepeth upon the earth after his kind: and God saw that it was good." The phrase of importance here is *after his kind.* Here we see that God made the beasts of the earth after "their kind." This verse tells us that dogs begot dogs, cows begot cows, and goats begot goats. This again is momentous and fundamental to our perception of who we are and who we belong to. Since we know that we are not beasts of the earth, it is imperative that we do not allow any comparison of our person to that of a beast.

Now let us move on to Genesis 1:26: "And God said, Let us make man in our image, after our likeness." Here, God created man in both his image and likeness. The terms *image* and *likeness* are synonymous and refer primarily to man's spiritual resemblance to his maker. To fully comprehend the interpretation of this verse, we must have an understanding of who and what God is.

No one can fully understand God; we know this, yet we allow ourselves to be seduced by lies and self-delusion because we believe that we do not have the strength or courage to look past what is temporal and fragile to aspire to what is eternal. Many people purchase big-ticket items like a home with big mortgages they know they cannot afford. As a result, when the first financial challenge appears, they panic. Why? They did not trust that they had the strength and courage to go the godly route, which is more rigorous. They feared that abundance would pass them by, and they were not powerful enough to gain what was real by virtue of their own strength. All this drama is due to a fear of failure. Today I am here to tell you a secret: You cannot fail.

Taking the heavenly path does demand strength and discipline. You must train yourself to set aside what you see and what seems to be wealth, for wealth is of the mind, as the highest form of currency is the mind. Then you must gradually teach your will to do as God's will does: Imagine in your mind's eye what you desire and allow the energies of the universe to accumulate and bring that goal into being. This is not easy to do, but it is truly not beyond the ability of any of you reading this book. We are all God's children and his surrogates in this world, and he would not have made the least of us without the potency to manifest what is good and just. However, if you lack the courage to take the enlightened path because you fear failure, then self-delusion and fleeting, empty achievements will be your reward. Remember, you cannot fail.

Precision begets honesty, and honesty begets courage; and all of these require faith. Once you perceive the truth about an aspiration or opportunity, you cannot be deceived again. Truth cannot become untrue. Simplicity, clarity, and single-mindedness give your life power, vividness, and joy because they are also the marks of great art. They seem to be the purpose of God for his whole creation. Without faith, all works are dead. Faith is inner confidence in things unseen. I am not talking about the childish faith that some people exhibit when they speak about God. Know this: God is infinitely more complex and subtle, as is the type of faith I'm referring to. Self-delusion bespeaks a weak or nonexistent faith in the ways of God and a refusal to believe that the principles of the self-fulfilling mind can actually be real. It is also a refusal to visualize a desire; focus the mind on that desire while shifting the essence of one's being to become that desire, and then allow the wheels of the divine to turn and bring that desire into one's experience.

There is a story about a man and his wife who aspired to buy a home for their family in a neighborhood that was beyond their means. In the beginning, they decided to let their desire come to them. They adhered to the principles of the mind, focused on their desire, remained courageous, and trusted that in time, when they were ready, their dream home would come into their lives. However, there is no knowing when God's system will act on your behalf. Some desires come about very quickly, but others can take years. Because of this, you must understand that your desire will only come when you are morally, emotionally, and spiritually ready to receive it. The ecology within must line up with the desired outcome. For example, you might desire a mansion, but if you are not ready for it, you might let it fall into disrepair or allow it to inflate your ego.

As time went by, the couple did not see their dream coming closer, and they slowly lost faith. They understood that they had to be ready to receive this gift, but they assumed that they were already ready, thereby valuing their judgment over God's. In doing this, they lost faith. Nonetheless, had they maintained their mental discipline, they would have brought about their objective. Instead, they pursued a desperate solution, lied about their income, and bought far more home than they could afford, and within a year, they were in financial trouble. Their loss of faith caused them to care only about the immediate circumstances and ignore the big picture. They had to be the people who were worthy of the gift before the gift came to them. When we lose faith, we lose faith not only in God's system, but also in ourselves as keepers of his will.

God Is Omnipotent
It is unattainable for our human minds to conjure up the vastness of God. The scriptures tell us that God is infinite. God is love. God is omnipotent. God is the beginning and the end. God is all in all. God is. However, we can understand God's laws and systems. This is compulsory since God made us in his image and after his likeness. Thus if we have some understanding of the Father, we will have some understanding of the sons and daughters of God. To put it simply, God is spirit. If God is spirit, then we are spirit. That is what Genesis 1 is telling us: "And God said, let us make man in our image, after our likeness."

To further our understanding of the God within, we come to one of God's basic principles: compensation. Compensation is continually ticking away to maintain that balance and harmony despite the chaotic nature of human life on this physical plane. That means that when something exits your life, you do not get to choose whether something else will come to fill that void! Compensation ensures that it will in accordance with the structure of the universal law that God laid down at the creation. You cannot get a pass from this; as soon as you lose a relationship or even a possession, the gears and machinery begin pulsing and turning to bring something else into your awareness. Whether or not you want it, this will happen. The principle of compensation consistently brings something into your experience to replace something that has left. It is regularly functioning and always waiting. It is impossible for it not to fill that void with some kind of freshly manifested potential, relationship, or reality.

Although you are personally responsible to govern the power of your divine mind to manifest your thoughts as reality at all times, this responsibility becomes especially keen when a void appears in your life. *That emptiness is temporary.* The great engine of universal creation will turn out some unknown thing or experience to keep your life balanced, so at this time more than any other, you must discipline and order your thoughts and focus them on creating abundance, health, and prosperity. It is impossible for the universe not to bring something fresh into your world. The principle of compensation works its wonders, whether you want it to or not.

For example, during these difficult financial times, you may lose your home to foreclosure, a terrible and humiliating ordeal to endure. However, in the wake of that loss, you don't respond by wrenching your mind into a hopeful and productive state. Instead, you choose to lie dormant. You retreat from the reality of what has happened in search of a "break" from the harshness of your situation. In doing so, you are like a driver who takes his hands off the wheel of a car going 140 kilometers per hour. You are abdicating any control over what happens.

Even inviting negative consequences into your experience is better than inviting chaos by refusing to think about the loss and what comes next. The universe will fill the void. If you don't fill it with the product of your imagination, the new influence in your life will come about from the thoughts and intentions of the people around you. Ask yourself: Would you rather trust your God-created mind to shape your future or the random—perhaps poisonous—thoughts of those around you?

You Are Spirit
We talked about the Bible verse that states that God made us in his image and likeness. An image is a representation or replica of one person or thing by another. The term *likeness* refers to a gauge of comparison, or analogy. So here we have a partial answer to our first question about who we are. According to the book of Genesis, we are spirit. It is imperative that we fully understand this. Here is a thought worth considering: If your imagination is Christ Jesus and all things are possible to Christ Jesus, are all things possible to you?

When you are able to grasp that you are spirit in a human body, then you will awaken to your true potential. You will know that you control the outside forces rather than them controlling you. If your mind remains firmly focused on manifesting the thing that recently left your experience, you can be sure you will find it coming back into your life. On the other hand, if you let your mental energies "float" without purpose or intent, then you may attract something rather different from what you knew. In other words, this is not some celestial photocopy service; it's not "lose a job, gain a job" unless you have a powerful and unrelenting desire to make it so. The key is this: What enters your experience to fill a vacuum tends to be whatever best serves your role in God's purpose at the time.

The specifics of the unknown influence often vary; you may lose a job and gain a family heirloom, or lose some aspect of your health to disease but gain a fresh purpose in helping others with the same disease. The principle of compensation is sometimes not direct (i.e., one thing for an identical thing). Very frequently, what enters your awareness to maintain the balance will be something in another area of life. So a job might compensate you for a lost relationship, or a new spiritual awareness might come to you in compensation for losing employment.

The *nature* of the compensatory force that enters your life, however, will never change. Its fundamental nature will match the tuning and frame of your divine mind in perfect harmony, for better or worse. After you suffer a layoff from your job, if you focus your attention on poverty and depression, then even a new relationship that may come in compensation will be based on poverty and depression. On the other hand, if you are diagnosed with cancer and have to lose part of your body in an effort to cure it, something else will arrive in your experience as compensation. If your mental force is beneficial, purposeful, and life-affirming, whatever form that new thing takes will also be favorable, determined, and life-affirming. The form can be different, but the status of your mind always determines the nature.

"Know ye not that your body is the temple of the Holy Ghost which is in you, which ye have of God and ye are not your own?" (1 Corinthians 6:19)

Our Bodies Are Temples of the Holy Ghost

As members of the human race, we give power to people and their words, especially those whom we believe are in a position of power. All the while, we are forgetting that a great power is sleeping within us. "Your body is the temple of the Holy Ghost" (1Corinthians 8:19). Not only is the local church a temple of the Holy Spirit, but the individual believer's body itself is also a temple of the Holy Spirit. You are spirit; however, in order to function on earth, you are encapsulated in human flesh. What is this mortal body? Why was it manifested? What do the scriptures say about the human body?

In 1 Corinthians, the Bible tells us that our bodies are temples of the Holy Ghost. This is an awesome revelation. Your body is the temple of the Holy Ghost. Pause and reflect on that statement for a moment. Let the revelation of what it means to you consume your very being. In essence, just relax and soak it all in. Take some deep breaths and contemplate what this means to you. We see further acknowledgment of this in 2 Corinthians 6:16: "And what agreement hath the temple of God with idols? For ye are the temple of the living God; as God hath said, I will dwell in them, and walk in them; and I will be their God, and they shall be my people."

Second Corinthians 6:16 goes much deeper. Here it states, "As God hath said, I will dwell in them, and walk in them." This once again supports the concept of you being a walking and talking spirit. God said he will walk and dwell in you. Here the words of God clearly establish that the human body is the temple of the Holy Ghost. So what are you doing with your inward power with respect to compensation?

There are two primary ways to leverage the principle of compensation. First, you must train your mind to set aside impulsive feelings of grief and anger over temporal losses. These feelings are products of the limited physical body manifesting its native attachment to the things of the flesh. You don't want to give up your comforts and the familiar, which is why change is so heart-wrenching. However, if you can remember that all things come to you via the grace of God's system, you will see that all things are temporary and designed to serve a greater good, which is your development into a superior vessel as part of God's divine design. Everything comes into and leaves your life at a prescribed time and for an ordained reason, though the webs may be so complex that you cannot perceive that reason.

You can develop this understanding primarily through prayer and meditation. It is important to develop your own discipline that will allow you to quiet your conscious mind and tap into the spirit level of consciousness, which reveals the flow of energy that is always waiting to manifest in your experience. Train your mind to focus on this energy and the eternal nature of the God in you. This will help you put the petty losses and gains of physical life in perspective and remember, even in dark times, that when you think God had to close a door, he inevitably opens a window.

The second way to develop a powerful adeptness with the principle of compensation is simply to review the times in your life when you have suffered losses and examine what results came from your mindset following the loss. Everything comes into your life for your greater good. It may not seem so at the time. However, in retrospect, you will see all the dots coming together.

2

Abundance is Your Inheritance

"I am come that they might have life, and that they might have it more abundantly."
(John 10:10)

Infinite Supply...It's Yours!
Abundance is yours. You cannot be deprived of God's supply. No one can take away what God has ordained for you. If you observe the lavish wastefulness of nature, you can discern that the Father intended for his children to be abundantly supplied, to lack for nothing, and to want for nothing. As Jesus says in Matthew 6:28–29: "Consider the lilies of the field, how they grow; they toil not; neither do they spin: And yet I say unto you, that even Solomon in all his glory was not arrayed like one of these."

As Christians, we know and understand this scripture, yet all too often, good, God-fearing people find themselves living from paycheck to paycheck. Why is that? We seem to have a morbid fascination with debt. Since we are now awakened to the truth of who we are, let us first address our responsibility to the kingdom. This fascination we have with debt is a dangerous game because in focusing on earthly debt, we ignore the universal debt that we must pay in life. That debt consists of obligations that we owe to the universe in return for the things it grants us. To whom much is granted, much is expected. "But he that knew not, and did commit things worthy of stripes, shall be beaten with few stripes. For unto whomsoever much is given, of him shall be much required: and to whom men have committed much, of him they will ask the more" (Luke 12:48). We are no exception. The blessings that God has given us are not free; we must pay for them in ways that have nothing to do with money. Even so, the mechanics behind earthly debt and spiritual debt have their similarities.

The story of Abraham is an excellent illustration of the concept of spiritual debt. Abraham was willing to sacrifice his beloved son Isaac to God because he felt the obligation of obedience. Abraham was well aware that he owed literally everything—even his very being—to God, and that therefore, he had an enormous debt to repay. He knew that if he did not repay it on God's terms as an act of his own free will, he would have to pay the debt in another way over which he had no control and that the consequences might be dire indeed. So he took his son to the mountain, bound him, and prepared to sacrifice him as a burnt offering. In the face of crippling emotional agony, Abraham's knowledge that he must repay his debt was all-powerful, and his determination to fulfill that obligation was the key.

Then on the third day Abraham lifted up his eyes, and saw the place afar off. And Abraham said unto his young men,

Abide ye here with the ass; and I and the lad will go yonder and worship, and come again to you. And Abraham took the wood of the burnt offering, and laid it upon Isaac his son; and he took the fire in his hand, and a knife; and they went both together. And Isaac spake unto Abraham his father, and said, My father: and he said, Here am I, my son. And he said, Behold the fire and the wood: but where is the lamb for a burnt offering? And Abraham said, My son, God will provide himself a lamb for a burnt offering: so they went both together. (Genesis 22:4–8)

In the scripture you just read, you will observe two things: First, Abraham said to his men, "I and the lad will go yonder and worship, and come again to you," meaning that in his mind's eye he saw both himself and Isaac returning. The second observation is Abraham's statement, "God would provide himself a lamb for a burnt offering." We can only speak about what we have already envisioned. As we know, the angel of the Lord stopped Abraham from slaying his son and God rewarded him for his faith and trust:

The angel of the Lord called to Abraham from heaven a second time and said, "I swear by myself, declares the Lord, that because you have done this and have not withheld your son, your only son, I will surely bless you and make your descendants as numerous as the stars in the sky and as the sand on the seashore. Your descendants will take possession of the cities of their enemies, and through your offspring, all nations on earth will be blessed, because you have obeyed me." (Genesis 22:15)

Only we are to blame when the fruit of the Spirit fails to appear in our life. All blessings come from God. However, we cannot manipulate God, force him, or pressure him to receive his blessings. We have the power to command happiness in our lives. When you know the truth of your being, you will no longer hinder the goodness of God from coming to you. You are a child of the Spirit, and every attribute of God and of good is your inheritance. You must accept and expect the fact that only you can make life happy and worthwhile for you. At most, the lack of faith can keep your good from reaching you. You must hold on to that truth.

In these turbulent economic times, many of us have the misfortune of watching not only our own futures made vulnerable, but also those of the people around us. And as so often proves true, the unenlightened are the victims not only of outside influence, but also of their own toxic minds, which attract into their paths the lack and misfortune upon which their thoughts reside. It is painful to watch others fall prey to their lack of understanding; they are their own mischievous sprite, not some outside rascal born in biblical myth. However, do not lose hope, for there is much we can do. Each person is the captain of his or her own soul, and so one can ultimately only save oneself.

Nevertheless, each of us has a duty not only to see to our own enlightenment within God's economic system, but to shepherd others in much the way that a financial custodian manages the affairs of his or her clients. When someone in your circle, community, or church is suffering from a loss, remind that person to fix his or her mind on possibility and creation, and remind the person that the principle of compensation is already at work knitting the fabric of reality into a new manifestation. This is how we can prevent those we love and cherish from falling repeatedly into the same traps! Patterns of thinking, after all, produce patterns of manifestation; this is why individuals who chronically lose their jobs seem to bounce from situation to situation, constantly sabotaging their own fortunes.

In fact, I believe that part of the principle of compensation may be that the more you repeat the same type of loss-to-compensation cycle, the more you reinforce the nature of your compensation. So the more often you respond to something exiting your life with a mental position of hope, empowerment, and creativity, the easier it may become for the universe to manifest good and abundance in your experience. Obviously, the reverse may also be true. The self-reinforcing nature of compensation means that we owe it to our fellow travelers on this physical plane to help them train their minds to enhance and grow their beings in the wake of loss. This can be as simple as reminding someone that loss is often a gateway to a finer good and to finer fortunes.

We must also remember that concern for our own welfare and prosperity should not blind us to our social obligations or spiritual destinies. A society in which individuals are concerned only about material welfare will not be able to achieve harmony and peace. Our obligations to God are not about material blessings, but spiritual ones. But what are some of our blessings, and how must we repay them? I see my life as both a gift and a responsibility. My responsibility is to use what God has given me to help his people in need. This, to me, is my primary obligation and repayment.

Nonetheless, we cannot control the blessings of God. God will manifest his blessings according to our faith in him. However, we are to prepare a place for the blessings and make sure that we are walking in divine order. That is it. That is all we have to do. It is not by the sweat of your brow but by the way that you think that you receive blessings. Your thought process can either hinder you or move you forward. Revelation 3:20 says, "Behold, I stand at the door, and knock: if any man hears my voice, and opens the door, I will come in to him, and will sup with him, and he with me."

Who is the "I" who stands at the door, and at what door is the "I" standing? Is the "I" yourself or the God who dwells within you? The "I" is God. The "door" is your consciousness. God-in-you stands at the door of your consciousness and knocks! You must open your mind (your consciousness) and admit him. The "I" is the bread of life (John 6:35). The "I" is the way, the truth, and the life (John 14:16). The "I" is the resurrection and the life (John 11:25). It is the "I" who comes that you might have life and have that life more abundantly (John 10:10). That "I" is standing at the door of your consciousness and knocking!

When you admit that "I" into your consciousness, you admit life eternal, the bread of life, the water of life, and the wine of life. You admit the power of the resurrection. When people hear the word *resurrection*, they often think of the resurrection of Jesus Christ. However, the Bible says that Christ lives in us (Romans 8:9). The Father knew you before you entered your mother's womb. When I refer to the resurrection, I am referring to the resurrection of your body, the resurrection of your home, the resurrection of your marriage, the resurrection of your good fortune, the resurrection of your business, and the resurrection of your dreams.

When you admit the "I" into your consciousness, only then do you admit the sacredness of life. When you acknowledge that the "I" in the midst of you is mighty, you are not speaking of a human being. You are speaking of the great "I Am," God himself. Pause and close your eyes for a minute, and within yourself, silently, sacredly, and gently affirm, "I." Say it until you can feel the power of it. The "I" that is in the midst of you is mighty. The "I" that is in the midst of you is greater than any problem in the outside world. The "I" that is in the midst of you has come that you might have life and have it more abundantly. The "I" has been with you since before Abraham was, awaiting your recognition and your acknowledgment.

"Know ye not that you are the temple of God?" (1 Corinthians 6:15). Do you not know that the name of God is "I" or "I Am" and that you are the temple of God? When you have admitted "I" into your consciousness and held it there secretly, sacredly, gently, and peacefully so that you can close your eyes and just remember it at any time, you will experience the true power of God in your life and the infinite blessings and abundance that are rightfully yours and that come as a result of your faith. You must affirm, "The 'I' in the midst of me is eternal. The 'I' that is within me is mighty."

The Christ Within

When a path to prosperity appears before you that seems easy and seems to require little or no sacrifice or spiritual development on your part, it is virtually certain to be an illusory path that will lead to nothing but frustration, wasted effort, and disappointment. The disciplined mind is the gateway to the abundance that Christ within grants us. Galatians 2:20 says, "I am crucified with Christ: nevertheless, I live; yet not I, but Christ liveth in me: and the life which I now live in the flesh I live by the faith of the Son of God, who loved me, and gave himself for me."

In Galatians 2:20, when Paul speaks of the Christ who dwells in him, he is referring to the "I Am"—the very "I" that you are and the "I" that is in the midst of you. However, you must avoid egotism and learn to differentiate between the egotistical "I" and the "I" in the midst of everyone. The egotistical "I" believes it has power and sufficient wisdom to rule the world or even just to run its own life. But the "I" in the midst of everyone is gentle, sacred, and powerful. To resist the egotistical "I," you must recognize that you cannot use or influence God. By yielding to the divine "I," God can use you.

When you focus your divine mind on the manifestation of a certain type of prosperity from the invisible substance of the universe, the process does not end there. It only begins. The universe is not a machine that simply sends you what you want at the push of a button. It is a mirror that reflects who you are in the act of becoming and brings forth a prosperity result in concordance with the discipline that you exhibit while your thought is taking form. So when you "think prosperity into your life," the result of that process will directly reflect the discipline you show after your thoughts initially project into the spiritual plane. Remember we are discussing the Christ within.

So let me ask you this: Do you continue to think about abundance and refuse to allow defeatist thinking to pollute your mind? Do you continue to work to the best of your ability without worrying about the results? Do you maintain your intention to use your coming prosperity for the greater good? Do you carry on with assisting others, acting with honor and rejecting relationships with people who do not do so? All these choices produce wealth because they color the type of prosperity the universe will bring forth into your corporeal world. The more diligent you are in your work, the more generous your spirit, the more humble you are in the face of God, and the greater your prosperity will be in all areas.

You may be surprised to learn that you cannot influence God. It is only when you yield to the divine "I" within you that God will influence you, guide you, direct you, feed you, clothe you, and provide shelter for you. Your heavenly Father, the "I" that you are, knows that you need all these things. It is the Father's good pleasure to give you the kingdom (Luke 12:32). If the ego convinces you even for a moment that God is subject to your way, remember quickly that it is not your will that will be done, but God's will. God's will can be done only to the degree of your yielding to the "I" within you.

You are walking in the Spirit of God. You have that Spirit of God within you. You know that there is a supreme being. There is a power greater than yourself! You are spirit. As Genesis 2:4–5 says, "The LORD God made the earth and the heavens, and every plant of the field before it was in the earth, and every herb of the field before it grew."

Growth Starts with a Purpose

The "I Am" in us is here for a purpose, and that purpose is to grow us, not to shrink us. That growth starts with a purpose. In essence, purpose is the engine and the power that drives and directs our lives. Using the power of the "I Am," we intentionally and mentally bring into our experience what we desire as if it were already manifest in our lives. The divine purpose is like a binding agent that lends our prosperity permanence. Our prosperity is like a temperamental plant in a garden; if it is tended and fed properly, it will take root and endure for many years. Even so, if it is neglected, it will wither and die long before its appointed lifespan is over. In this way, a true desire is not to have, but to be. We are whole creatures in potential, and the true purpose of desire is to unfold that wholeness, to become what we can be.

Johann Wolfgang von Goethe once said, "Desire is the presentiment of our inner abilities and the forerunner of our ultimate accomplishments." We must remember, however, that we must use wealth as granted through God's system to serve our individual, unique purposes. If we do not, the wealth is temporary. It will not and cannot last.

Proverbs 24:3–4 reads: "Through wisdom is a house built; and by understanding it is established. And by knowledge shall the chambers be filled with all precious and pleasant riches." To acquire lasting wealth, we must know and understand God's purpose for the wealth, for there is no wealth without purpose.

There is a spiritual principle guiding our heavenly purpose; ignoring that divine purpose and using prosperity exclusively for self-directed goals will interrupt the existence of that wealth in the future. The wealth will either depart or not come in the first place. In other words, if you wish to realize lifelong prosperity, you must know and serve God's purpose. As Proverbs 13:11 states, "Dishonest money dwindles away, but he who gathers money little by little makes it grow."

This does not mean that you must turn your fine home into a shelter for the homeless; generous deeds are not automatically in tune with the purpose God has in mind for you. It is a myth that all divine deeds must involve selfless giving and charity must be without reward. In truth, many kinds of deeds serve the divine purpose. Some may indeed be unselfish and generous, but others may involve entrepreneurship and creating jobs, running for political office, engaging in an ascetic spiritual study, building a facility for people in the community, or even writing books or music that inspires others. There are many ways to serve God with wealth.

3

ARE WE VICTIMS OF CIRCUMSTANCES?

"Every man also to whom God hath given riches and wealth, and hath given him power to eat thereof, and to take his portion, and to rejoice in his labor; this is the gift of God."
(ECCLESIASTES 5:19)

MANY PEOPLE WONDER whether a person has the capacity, equipment, and power to control his life—whether he can be what he wants to be or whether he is a drop in the great ocean of life. Unemployment, poverty, and want impact millions. Can they help it? Can people really repair broken homes and family problems? Millions complain of sickness and disorder in countless forms. All this gives rise to the belief that we are victims of circumstances over which we have no control. However, such beliefs make us fatalists instead of masters of our own destinies.

Do not buy into that belief system. Fatalism is contagious. When people submit to the influence and beliefs of a fatalist and start to think that the circumstances around them are stronger than the power within them, they are defeated before they start. If you think that the outside conditions are greater than what is in you, you are dead before you even start living.

The history of mankind contains overwhelming evidence of people overcoming circumstances and meeting challenges in life. Evolution and anthropology support the truth that people are responsible for their conditions. We have the power to control our circumstances. By using this power, we create the circumstances necessary for our upward climb. However, some people do not believe that we create our circumstances and are prone to think that their problems and challenges are hereditary or a result of karma, the environment, or numerous other external factors.

They blame the external factors for their failures in life. They believe in the natural limitation of life. They are always unsure where they are and what they will become. If you are one of these people, you must change this type of belief system. You must eradicate the belief that you are a victim of your environment, your color, your race, or where you were born if you want to break the cycle of limitation and lack in your life and move forward.

Evolution and anthropology tells us that man is responsible for what he is. The scientists on the other hand, searching the mysteries of life, reveal to us a wonderful world of power, possibilities, and promise. They tell us that our minds are the creative cause of all results in our lives, that personal conditions are the result of our actions, and that our actions are the direct result of our ideas. You never make a move of any kind until you first form some kind of image, plan, or idea in your mind. These images, plans, and ideas are powerful and potent. They are the cause (good, bad, or indifferent) of the subsequent effects, which in turn correspond to their natures. Scientists believe that these ideas generate tremendous energy. Hence, when we learn to employ our minds constructively, we use these hidden powers, forces, and faculties correctly. According to scientists, this is the key to successful living.

However, in the spiritual realm, there is a marvelous inner world that exists within us. The revelation of such a world enables us to attain and achieve anything we desire within the bounds or limits of nature. If everyone has the power and privilege to determine his or her fortune, how do we identify this inner power? If all conditions result from our actions and our actions are the fruit of our ideas, then our ideas must determine the conditions of our daily lives. Given all the above reasoning, the question still remains: How do we know our authentic purpose? Or in other words, why are we here?

Follow Your Passion
How do you discover your purpose, and how do you know that you are following it? The response to the first question is astonishingly straightforward: Follow your passion. God imbues each of us at creation with one or more pure, flaming passions—desires to follow a path that may have nothing to do with what our families wish for or what we want to do to make a certain amount of money. These passions are often buried, but they cannot be silenced. They propagate within us throughout our lives, immortal and impossible to ignore. Passion is God's purpose singing within us. Passion drives us to face any obstacle, turn over the previous structure of our lives, and endure years of hardship to do what we feel we are meant to do.

Where do you think such an uncontrollable desire comes from? It can only come from one source: the Spirit of God burning in us. God created our spirits with a purpose in mind, and each purpose is a small piece in the great riddle of evolving human existence. Because God is pure spirit, he cannot act in the physical world; thus, we are his surrogates. Each of us plays a small but crucial role in the physical realization of God's spiritual plan. Everyone is important in this. Even the smallest bolt in a great suspension bridge may cause disaster if it fails; likewise, each man and woman has a life-sustaining purpose. So when we listen to and obey that passion that speaks to us in the middle of the night and calls us to do things that may seem insane in the light of day, we are truly in the center of divine purpose.

Now passion does not always ask us to do things that destroy what we have built, such as selling a successful business to pursue a life of impoverished preaching. Sometimes the price will be this high; other times it will be lower. Purpose and passion are different for everyone. Nevertheless, they have one essential factor in common, something all of us must remember: God will always call you to a purpose whose primary function is to inspire others to evolve spiritually and find the divine in themselves.

This is amazingly important. All passion is designed to guide us toward decisions and pursuits that eventually help our brothers and sisters discover their personal passions and their particular supernatural minds! This is why godlike purpose can take so many different forms. For some individuals, it may be pure giving and devotion to helping the oppressed, but in others, it might be working to preserve nature, playing a sport, or launching a business. However, in the wholeness of God's vision, each activity born of pure passion serves a goal: inspiring those who witness it to grow in spirit and take their own places in God's purpose. So when you hear God's voice speaking to you in a passion that gnaws at your soul, listen to it. Do not deny it. When left unattended, passion blights life and happiness, leaving us empty and hollow. Instead, realize that when you are living your passion, wealth will come to you so that you may better inspire others to discover and pursue their own passions!

The answer to the other part of this question—about knowing if you are in the center of God's purpose for you—comes from a careful and honest observation of your life and fortunes. Adherence to purpose is a self-fulfilling machine of manifestation. If your prosperity is in line with the divine purpose, you will find that your "I Am" desire for greater prosperity will increase your wealth. However, if you ignore your passion and thus God's purpose, then you will not only find that new wealth is impossible to come by, but that the wealth you have also seems to be slipping away.

The Creative Power of the Mind

It is tempting to assume that once the prosperity we desire has appeared in our lives via the conduit of our divine minds, we can become consumed by it, abandon our disciplined ways, and not worry about the consequences. However, nothing could be further from the truth. In fact, the act of our own transformation and the act of divine manifestation are the same; both are evolutionary processes that have no stopping point. Because prosperity is a process of becoming, not a delivery system that simply drops wealth on your doorstep, you must continue to exercise intimate discipline to keep what you have gained. To understand this further, let's address the creative power of the mind.

An idea is a thought or a group of thoughts, an image, or a picture in the mind. There is an idea or a mental picture behind every well-known achievement or invention. The mind has the creative power. From the beginning of time, the great architect, God himself, has implemented this creative power, as outlined in the first book of the Bible. God had a pattern and a plan for growth. He had an idea that grew. The creator's mind established a mental picture before creation itself became a reality.

The Lord God made the earth and the heavens and every plant in the field before it was on the earth. Everything must be created in spirit. That is the truth of who you are. You have to go to the source. Stop fighting over the spoils in life; those are effects. Go to the source for everything that you need. Go to the source to implement your creative power. You have the infinite source, the source that never dries up, living inside you. Go to the source for everything. You have to learn to go within yourself to create what you need in your natural experience.

Every architect follows a plan, whether he is building a house, a bridge, an institution, or his own life. Every man is his own designer and builder. Like the creator, we make our creations within, before they materialize on the outside. All fears of sickness, poverty, old age, and depression are mental pictures and ideas long before they become some painful reality. No one wants to inflict pain and suffering on themselves. However, when we allow negative thoughts to overshadow the creative power of our minds, then we are subjecting ourselves to pain. As Proverbs 23:7 says, "For as he thinks in his heart, so is he."

Gloomy self-talk, pessimistic self-images, and cynical feelings can lead to self-destruction. To combat these things, it is paramount to begin to build what Neuro-Linguistic Programming (NLP) calls a "rapport" with yourself. Rapport means congruency with someone or something, or a close, harmonious relationship. When you say you are in a rapport with something or someone, it means that you are congruent with the person or thing.

As humans, we experience life through our five senses: sight, hearing, touch, smell, and taste. According to NLP teachings, cynical thoughts attack our three main sensory receivers: auditory, visual, and kinesthetic. Pessimistic self-talk relates to auditory receivers; negative self-images relate to visual receivers; and feelings of negativity relate to kinesthetic receivers. Negative thoughts form patterns, and those patterns form your belief system.

If you are not experiencing the abundant life that God has commissioned for you, you must change your belief system. You have to guard the gate of your mind more closely. Nobody is exempt from cynical thinking, gloomy self-talk, pessimistic self-images, and uncooperative feelings about oneself. However, if you want to experience all that God has for you, you have to implement the techniques that will arrest these negative thoughts early so that they do not take root in your conscious mind and express themselves in your outside world as reality.

Every idea or mental picture must produce after its own kind, whether good, bad, or indifferent. It is the law of cause and effect. The law of cause and effect does not question or challenge a person's mental pictures, images, and thoughts. It takes what the person plants and materializes it into a visual form. Some people can visualize great engineering achievements. However, many are not aware that by using the duplicate technique of visualization, they can overcome sickness and disease in their own bodies. The interchangeable visualization techniques used to picture a house or create a portrait are the identical techniques used to visualize you perfect and whole. It's the equivalent principle.

A picture of a homely person never develops into a picture of a beautiful pageant winner, and a short person does not look tall in a photograph. A picture will only mirror the image projected. There is a story of a woman who once lived in a beautiful home in an exclusive suburban area. She was happy. She had every comfort imaginable. The home was large and had a fence, a beautiful lake, and a nice flower garden. She had servants to help her maintain the property. She was living the life of which many people could only dream. However, she began to say within herself, "I don't need this big house. All I want is a little room for myself. That's all I need. This house is too large. All I want is a little room, a little place that I could just keep clean."

A few years later, her husband died and left her the estate. She sold the house. Unfortunately, because of the downward spiral in the economy, her other holdings and investments diminished in value to nothing. Unable to rebound financially, she was forced to rent a small room in someone else's home. What she had visualized in her mind over time became her reality.

As we assimilate the negative ideas and mental pictures, we consciously and sometimes unconsciously exercise our power to produce them. This creative process continues working night and day until the idea is completed. We cannot picture thoughts of poverty, failure, disease, and doubt and expect to experience wealth, success, health, and courage. Your outward picture will always represent your inward thoughts. As Proverbs 23:7 says, "As a man thinks in his heart, so is he."

Building Rapport Within
As you move forward in life and dismantle the negative thoughts in your mind, you must develop a rapport with yourself. You must be congruent with your thoughts. If you are not able to develop congruency with your thoughts, you will block your blessings. To

maximize effective communication with others, you must have a good relationship with yourself. In other words, you should have a rapport with yourself. Our natural state is to be in rapport with ourselves. However, as we grow older, we lose this connection. We become more self-conscious, which results in self-assessment.

Negative self-assessment—whether visual, auditory, or kinesthetic—is detrimental to experiencing and exercising individual power. If you give credence to unwilling self-talk, cynical self-images, or negative feelings of yourself, you adversely impact your private power. You hinder your God-self. You self-impose limitations that cause you to be stagnant. You interrupt your natural state, and in doing so, you block rapport with yourself.

Negative self-talk is one of the most insidious ways we block rapport and sabotage ourselves. It results in personal misery. When you hear yourself entering into condemning self-talk, you should immediately stop, pull yourself out of its unfavorable spiral, and begin to reframe your thoughts. One simple strategy for doing this is to say "Stop" aloud as soon as you hear these thoughts. This will interrupt the disadvantageous self-talk and give you an opportunity to deal with your doubtful thoughts. Give yourself a pep talk. Don't have a pity party. Just stop the negative self-talk in its tracks.

Negative self-images are another detriment to our distinctive power. We sometimes deplete our particular power by dwelling on these images. We see in our mind's eye previews of "coming attractions," and the movies are often not pleasant ones. How do we turn off this preview? How do we turn on the movies that will give us the pleasant realities? In order to have a more balanced life, I started playing golf. I play once a week on Wednesday, as that is ladies' night. I am not a very good golfer; nevertheless, I like the game. On this particular Wednesday, I teed off with a very pleasant shot on a par three and landed near the hole. Looking for a ball marker to mark my ball, I found that I did not have any. One of the other women told me to use hers. Right away, I could hear the little voice in my head start telling me that I would be a nuisance to these ladies, for I would have to keep borrowing their ball marker. I knew I had to interrupt that negative self-talk. So I said within myself, "Stop it, you are not a bother." I subsequently came up with the resolution that next week I would bring a ten-cent coin and use that until I obtained a ball marker at the golf shop. I rested afterward in that conviction and continued playing.

Unbeknownst to me, that night was a trophy night, and at the seventh hole, I again landed on the green just inches from the hole. That hole was the reward hole, and my prize was a women's revolutionary professional high-performance glove with a ball marker attached. All this is to say that there was a need, and then self-doubt. I stepped in and rapidly interrupted the negative self-talk. As a result, the manifestation of the thing desired came quickly.

Neuro-Linguistic Programming teaches a powerful technique to reclaim the screening room of your mind. It is called the "swish pattern." You can reclaim the screening room in your mind. The thoughts in your head are like a movie. They are like a preview of a movie playing repeatedly. If you don't like the movie that is playing in your mind, you can change it. The swish pattern is like a picture in the future.

You may be familiar with the picture-in-picture feature in many televisions. This feature enables you to have two channels on the screen at the same time; one a large, full-screen picture and the other a smaller picture in the corner of the bigger picture. If something of greater interest appears on the smaller screen, you can then switch the image to the bigger screen.

You can implement this same technique when counterbalancing self-images that form in your mind. You can use the "swish pattern" to neutralize images that come to your mind. First, create a picture of a desired state, and then insert that desired state in the smaller window of your mental screen. In other words, the state that you desire goes into the small screen. This can be either a still image or a series of moving pictures. The negative image that is dominating your mind is not the one you want. Instead, swish (or switch) the screens so that you project your desire on the bigger screen of your mind.

As you swish the images, your ultimate objective is to have the positive image become most dominant in your mind. Assume the power to choose which channel you want to watch in your mind rather than allowing unwanted channels to beam insidiously in your internal deliberating processes. You are in control of the pictures in your mind, and it is therefore your choice which images are dominant. You have a choice. You do not have to suffer. As 2 Corinthians 10:5 says, "Casting down imaginations, and every high thing that exalteth itself against the knowledge of God, and bringing into captivity every thought to the obedience of Christ."

As you build rapport with yourself, your God-given passion will always have a positive effect on you and the world around you, though others may not understand it at first. Spending part of your free time helping others cannot possibly hurt anyone and will probably benefit you and others, making it an authentic passion and thus divine in origin. There is no way that any genuine passion can be out of line with God's purpose and your own manifestation of prosperity. If you are engaging in activities that uplift others with your wealth, that may be what God wishes you to do.

Affirmation
I want you to repeat the following affirmation, which will keep the negative self-talk, self-images, and feelings at bay and allow you to manifest the blessings of God in your life. Enter into a quiet, relaxed state. Become one with the Father within you. Put your feet flat on the ground. Take a deep breath in and out and repeat: "Father, within me is the infinite, limitless spiritual universe. Let it flow. Let it be the avenue to bring healing, feed the multitudes, and provide understanding, companionship, and aid. Let all of this flow as a service unto thee. In Jesus's mighty name, amen."

4

Claim Your Truth

"And ye shall know the truth, and the truth shall make you free."
(John 8:32)

Be Not Afraid...Success Is Your Birthright!

You cannot over commit your richness to the true works of God. It is simply impossible. When you are working in the Spirit and focused on a passion that is truly born of God, then no matter how much wealth, time, or knowledge you give away to others, more will flow into your hands as a result. It is impossible to become impoverished when you depend on God as your sole means of support.

"Fear thou not; for I am with thee: be not dismayed; for I am thy God: I will strengthen thee; yea, I will help thee; yea, I will uphold thee with the right hand of my righteousness" (Isaiah 41:10).

Frequently, in scripture, when the angel of the Lord appears, the first thing the angel says is, "Be not distressed," as in the verse above. You cannot be fearful to claim your truth. What is your truth? Did you know that success is your birthright? If a man constantly has thoughts of sickness, poverty, and misfortune, eventually he will encounter them in his life and claim them as his own. He will fail to acknowledge his close relationship with God. He will even deny his own children and declare they were sent to him by an evil fate. Even so, he refuses to accept that abundance and prosperity are his birthright. Unless he cannot help himself, no man has a right to remain constantly subjected to cramped ambition, blighted influence, and great temptations of poverty.

No man has a right to stay in that kind of an environment. His self-respect demands that he should get out of such an environment. It is his duty to put himself in a position of dignity and independence, where he will not be a burden on his friends or cause those depending on him to suffer.

The wealthy person will tell you that his greatest satisfaction and happiest days were when he was emerging from poverty into competency. He remembers when the pressure from his small savings started to swell into a stream of fortune, and he knew that want would no longer control his life. What a great feeling! It was then he began to experience leisure and self-development, or perhaps study, travel, and the relief that his loved ones would be free from the clutches of poverty. Comforts took the place of stern necessity and blundering drudgery. He realized that he had the power to lift himself above his current state, that he could have an impact on the world, that he would have the luxuries and comforts of life (movies, music, books), and that his children, unlike himself, would not have to struggle to receive a good education. He sensed the invigorating power of being able to give his children and others a start in the world and the satisfaction of watching his small circle of influence expand into a larger sphere, broadening into a wider horizon.

Lack and want do not fit our divine DNA. Scripture gives overwhelming evidence that God made us for grand and sublime things, for abundance and not for poverty. However, many people do not have enough faith to receive the good that God preordained for them from the beginning. Many dare not break away from their sole desire to follow the leading of their divine hunger and ask for the abundance that is their birthright. They ask for small, temporary blessings and expect miniscule rewards; they pinch their desires and limit their supply, not daring to ask for the fullness of their souls' desire. They refuse to open their minds sufficiently to allow the great inflow of good things into their lives. Their mentality is restricted with self-doubt and repressed to the point that they are stingy and limited. Many struggle to fling out their souls' desire with the abundant faith that trusts implicitly and receives accordingly.

The power that made and sustains us gives to everyone and everything liberally and abundantly, not stingily. There is no restriction, no limitation, and no loss to anyone as a result of God's abundant giving. The rose does not ask the sun for only a small portion of its light and heat. It is the sun's nature to give its energy to everything that will absorb it. The candle loses none of its light by lighting another candle. Likewise, the creator does not lack when he grants our requests. He does not have less because we ask for much. It is God's nature to give to his children and to flood us with our hearts' desires.

By being friendly and giving abundantly of our love, we do not lose but rather increase our capacity for friendship. One of the greatest secrets of life is to learn how to transfer the full current of divine force to ourselves and use this force effectively.

If a man can discover this law of divine transfer and apply it to his life, he will multiply his efficiency a millionfold. He will be a cooperator and a cocreator with the divine on a scale of which he has never before dreamed.

When we recognize that everything comes from the infinite supply (God) and flows through us freely, when we become perfectly in tune with the infinite, when we have outgrown dishonesty, selfishness, and impurity, then we will see God without the scales that blind us to our good. We shall see God. We shall see our good. We shall know our good. Only the pure in heart can see God (Matthew 5:8).

Divorcing Lack and Limitation
If you get rid of the desire to take advantage of your brothers and sisters, you will become so close to God that all the good in the universe will flow spontaneously to you. However, many people restrict the inflow of good throughout their lives by engaging in wrongful acts and thinking wrong thoughts. Every vicious deed is a veil—a film over our eyes so that we cannot see God—and, as a result, we are blinded from our good. Every wrong step separates us from God.

When you learn the art of seeing opulently instead of stingily, and when you learn to think without limits, refusing to let your own limiting thoughts cramp your potential, you will find that what you are seeking is also seeking you and will meet you halfway.

Do not apologize when lack decides to show up in your life, and do not continuously confess your lack of this or that. Every time you confirm that you have nothing fit to wear, that you do not have things that other people have, or that you never go anywhere or do things that other people do, you are simply etching this sad picture more deeply into your subconscious mind. As long as you recite these unfortunate details and dwell upon your disagreeable experiences, your mentality will not attract what you desire or the remedy to your difficult conditions.

Prosperity begins in the mind and is impossible to manifest in your life with a hostile attitude. Your mental picture must correspond to the reality that you seek. You cannot attract opulence if a poverty-stricken attitude and mentality drive you. It is fatal to work for one thing and expect something else. No matter how much you may long for prosperity, a miserable, poverty-stricken attitude will close all avenues to it. The weaving of the web is bound to follow the pattern. Opulence and prosperity cannot come through thoughts of poverty and failing thought channels. You create prosperity first in the mind, and then it will appear in your natural experience.

Many people live with the belief that the world has plenty of good things for others (e.g., comforts, luxuries, beautiful houses, fine clothing, opportunity for travel, leisure), but just not for them. They accept the conviction that these things do not belong to them but are for a different class of people. But why do these people think they are in a different class than people who have good things? Simply put, they think themselves into a place of inferiority. They place limits on themselves and accept the lie that good things are not for them.

Thoughts of inferiority, lack, and limitation cause you to erect barriers between you and having plenty. You cut off the flow of abundance to you and make the law of supply inoperable in your life by shutting your mind to it. By what law can you expect to get what you believe you cannot have? By what philosophy can you obtain the good things of the world when you are thoroughly convinced that they are not for you? Limitation is in man, not in the creator. The Father wants his children to have all the good things of the universe because he has fashioned these things for his own. If you do not allow the good of God to flow to you, you limit yourself.

One of the greatest curses in this world is the belief that poverty is necessary. Many people have a strong conviction that some people were born to be poor. However, there was no poverty, no wants, and no lack in the creator's plan for mankind. There should not be a poor person on the planet. The earth is full of resources that we hold secretly, yet scarcely touch. There is no lack, just lack of distribution. It is as if someone is keeping these resources a big secret.

People are poor in the midst of abundance simply because of their own limiting thoughts. Life incorporates the thoughts that we bring into it. If we fear poverty and want, our life texture incorporates these thoughts and causes us to attract more poverty. God never intended for us to have such a difficult time making a living, or to just to squeeze by to get a few more comforts, or to spend all of our lifetimes making a living instead of making a life. The abundant life, full, free, and beautiful, was intended for us. If we were absolutely normal, making a living would be a mere part of us making a life for ourselves.

The great ambition of the human race should be to develop a superb type of manhood and a beautiful, magnificent womanhood. We would focus on building up and forming people instead of making a dollar, as we see now. Resolve that you will turn your back on the poverty mentality, vigorously expect prosperity, and hold tenaciously to the thought of abundance and opulence. These are the things that befit your nature, so live in the realization of plenty so you can actually feel rich. This will help you to attain that which you long for.

We Are Heirs of All That He Is

There is a creative force and an intense desire for prosperity and abundance. We all live in our personal worlds. We are creations of our particular thoughts. Each person builds his own world by his thought habits. You have the choice to dwell in an atmosphere of abundance or lack, plenty or want. However, God did not create his children to grovel. He created us to aspire, to prosper, to have dominion, and to look up, not down. God did not make us to squeak by in poverty, but to acquire larger, grander things.

Nothing is too good for the children of the prince of peace. Nothing is as important or as beautiful as the sons and daughters of God. Nothing is too grand, too sublime, or too magnificent for us to enjoy. It is the poverty attitude and the narrowness of our thoughts that limit us. If we had a larger, grander conception of life and our birthright, we would live far more complete and fuller lives. Instead of whining, crawling, grumbling, sneaking, and apologizing, we ought to stand erect, claim our kingship, and demand our rightful inheritance, which is an abundance of everything that is good, beautiful, and true. As heirs of God, we should not be so poverty-stricken. However, the narrowness of our faith and our misconceptions of our true birthright causes many to miss their divine inheritance and to miss walking in the fullness and abundance of an unlimited supply.

Our environment provides vast evidence that God made us for infinitely grand and superb things that only the most fortunate seem to possess and enjoy. If we are God's children and made in God's image, why not expect great, grand things? We are heirs of all that he is, all that he has, and all that is beautiful and opulent in the universe. Those who expect and appreciate the wealth of God will obtain it.

Something is wrong when the sons and daughters of the king of kings choose to walk past all the good things of the universe that are their inheritance. Our circumstances in life, our financial conditions, our poverty or wealth, and our relationships are all the offspring of our thoughts. If you have had an attitude of want and lack, your environment will correspond. However, if you have had thoughts of abundance and prosperity and have tried to realize these conditions in your life, your environment will also correspond. Everything we receive in life comes through the gateway of our thoughts and resembles the quality of our thoughts. If our thoughts are pinching, stingy, and mean, we will see that in our natural experience.

Unless they have suffered ill health or some unusual misfortune, people who live in poverty for years are in sin because they are harboring the wrong attitudes. The head of this kind of household is often a complainer who believes that he is fated to have a small supply and inflow. If you are dissatisfied with your condition, or you feel that life has been hard and fate has been cruel, you will probably find that the condition of your home, business, or social life is the legitimate offspring of your own thoughts, ideas, and beliefs. You have no one to blame but yourself.

Exact thinking will produce correct living, clean thinking, a laundered life, and prosperous, generous thoughts. You will then start trying to make your thoughts and your ideals real, and those efforts will produce corresponding results. We will never know want if we learn to implicitly trust the great dispenser of all good, the source of infinite supply, the power that brings seedtime and harvest, and the one who generates our supplies. God is the power who bids us not to think of tomorrow but to consider how the lilies grow and how they live.

The human race lacks the unquestioned, implicit confidence in the divine source of all supplies. As heirs of God, we should stand in relation to the infinite source, as a child does to his parents. The child does not say, "I shouldn't eat this food because I may not get any more." Instead, he takes everything with absolute confidence and assurance that his parents will supply all his needs and that there is plenty more in the storehouse.

God intended for us to live the abundant life and to have plenty of everything that is good. However, many people are not aware of their possibilities. They do not expect enough of themselves. They do not demand sufficiently, so they receive only meagerness and stinginess. They do not demand the abundance that rightfully belongs to them, and so they end up with leanness, lack of fullness, and incompleteness in their lives. They do not demand the royalty that is due to them. They are content with too little.

No one was meant to live in poverty and wretchedness. Lacking anything desirable is not natural for any human being. Hold on to the thought that you are one with what you want. Be so in tune with what you desire that you attract it. Keep your mind vigorously concentrated upon it. Never doubt your ability to receive what you desire, and you will see it manifest in your world. Poverty is a mental disease. If you are suffering from it and are a victim of it, you will be surprised to see how quickly your condition improves when you change your attitude.

Remember, do not dwell on the miserable, shivering, limited poverty image, but turn around and face toward abundance, plenty, freedom, and happiness. Success comes through a perfectly scientific mental process. The man who becomes affluent does so because he first believed he was prosperous. He has faith in his ability to make money. He does not start out with his mind filled with doubt and fear. He does not constantly engage in conversations about poverty. He does not think about poverty. He does not live like a pauper. Instead, he turns his face toward what he is striving for; he is determined to receive it, and he will not admit any contrary picture in his mind.

Multitudes of poor people are satisfied with remaining in poverty and have ceased to struggle to rise out of it. They may work hard, but they have lost hope and the expectation that they will be free from poverty's clutches. Many people keep themselves poor because they intensely fear poverty and allow themselves to dwell on the possibility of falling into a state of want and lack. The minds of children in many families are saturated with thoughts of poverty. They hear conversations about poverty, lack, and limitation from morning until night. They see poverty-stricken conditions everywhere. Everything around them suggests poverty. Is it any wonder that children who grow up in such an atmosphere repeat the same poverty-stricken conditions as their parents?

Fear of poverty, constant worry about making ends meet, and fear of an awful, rainy day not only make you unhappy, but also add to a load that is already too heavy for you to bear. No matter how bleak the outlook or how unmovable your environment may seem, you ought to refuse to see anything that is unfavorable. Choose not to see any condition that intends to enslave you and keep you from expressing the best that you are. Positively refuse to do it and see what happens in your life.

There Is No Limit
God's word is true. However, many people try to conceal the main purpose of their lives. They tell all kinds of stories about what they are seeking. Often they confess that all they have is enough to feed, clothe, and house their families. Many say, "I don't want too much." That kind of thinking is not of God. That is not your truth. Those are your thoughts, not the thoughts of God.

Be honest about your pursuit of God's boundless bounty because that is what God has intended for you. Nothing will satisfy you but the unrestricted supply, for God is infinite supply. God is the very idea of limitless supply, but we keep this idea suppressed within our minds. Name your good. Confess your good! Declare your good! Do not fail to say, "My good is unlimited support," and you will see that good soon brings you marvelous support. New provisions will be made for you.

There is no limit to the bounty of truth. Any thoughts contrary to this truth are not the God-in-you speaking. That is the human you limiting God. God's truth is unlimited supply. Prosperity is sure to come to you when you speak the truth. Jesus says that all who learn his doctrine will receive a hundredfold more possessions in their lives. "But he that received seed into the good ground is he that heareth the word, and understandeth it; which also beareth fruit, and bringeth forth, some an hundredfold, some sixty, some thirty" (Mathew 13:23).

The scripture tells us to take no thought for ourselves but proclaim to the universe, My support is my God. My good is my God. God is my support

Stop muzzling God. Jesus says that in this life, we will have tribulations while receiving our good support, but he also said, "Be not afraid, I have overcome" (John 16:33). This is his word. He meant he has overcome the worldly ways of others supporting you by telling the truth, and he assures you that good will surely come to you. Tribulation is the opposition that we meet when we tell the world that we receive our support by thinking and speaking truth. Tribulation is the feeling we have when we start on the path that is exactly opposite of our former ways of thinking. Tribulation will come when we attempt to cast away all anxiety and give up trying to obtain our living through our old ways of thinking.

Every time God deposits a truth in you—whether it comes through the Spirit of God within you, a prophetic word, or even a child—you will immediately encounter tribulation. When you hear the truth that you are healed, you will encounter tribulation right away. Know that this is the way of life, but it must not move you off course. It must not sway you from your truth. The only way to receive God's truth is to speak it. As John 1:1 says, "In the beginning was the Word, and the Word was with God, and the Word was God."

You have to speak his truth. God is Good. God is substance. God is spirit. Therefore, your supply comes from spirit and as spirit. It is not tribulation to practice providing for you by telling the truth. After a little while, you won't have distress because you will know exactly how spirit works. However, right now, every time God deposits a truth in you, you look to materiality to support a spiritual truth. The two do not mix.

Do Not Be Afraid to Claim Your Truth
Receive your truth and eventually you will see it in material form. However, you first have to receive it. Many people fall into the trap of doubt before they receive their truth, and as a result, they do not speak it. They keep it silent and focus on the tribulation. Erroneously, they voice the tribulation. However, when you constantly focus on the tribulation, you are declaring that God's word will not come to pass. In fact, you never gave God's word a chance. You never spoke it. You did not recognize it.

Love, life, truth, substance, and intelligence are names of our good. Declare that your good is truth. This will cause your lips to speak the truth. There is no evil in good. God is good. Therefore, there is no evil in God and no evil in his good. When you speak your truth and mix it with evil, it is no longer your truth. Rather, it is something else that you are speaking. When God gives you a word, hold on to it and speak that truth.

As soon as we say, "God is not the author of sickness; God is good; excellence is truth; truth is God," we can no longer declare that sickness is good. Good is God; therefore, God is health. God is unbounded, unlimited love. God is our love. Because God loves us, he instinctively seeks all things for our good. When you say that God is love, he will guide you. A mother's soft kiss has literally saved lives. Many women have felt uplifted again when they hear the voices of their children calling their names.

My mother had Alzheimer's disease, and the doctors were counting down her last days. She didn't recognize anyone. When I went to see her, they kept telling her, "It's your daughter, Gloria."

I also said, "It's Gloria."

Finally, something got through, and she said, "My Gloria?" And with that, there was an awakening. That simple recognition from a cognitively damaged mind registered such a warm feeling in my heart, and it remains with me even today.

Do not underestimate the power of love. God is love. God is truth. Love is truth. Declare your truth: "The good I am seeking is love." No one can fully explain the heights and depths and splendor of love. God's love is so great that he personified it through his son Jesus. The little children came close to his knees; poor, neglected women followed him; the blind and the beggars clung to his clothes; and dignitaries came by night to speak with him. Love does not come to us by any one man, woman, or child and then go away. One person's affection is only a sign of love. God's love is eternal. God's love is infinite. As he says in Jeremiah 29:11, "For I know the thoughts that I think toward you, saith the Lord, thoughts of peace, and not of evil, to give you an expected end."

How can we attain our good? We cannot attain it by working with our hands for countless ages. We can only attain the fullness of God's good for our lives through the way of Jesus Christ. Jesus Christ is all truth. The Jesus Christ method brings the fulfillment of all experience. You must expect the good of God to manifest and overflow in your life. Have a clear idea of a sweet, free, and unburdened life. Visualize it. See it in your mind's eye. If you have a clear picture in your mind, you will be able to focus on the God within you and bring that life forward. However, you have to create the image in your mind first. You have to picture it and declare very plainly, "This sweet, free, unburdened life *is* my good."

Do not be afraid to claim your truth! Do not be frightened to claim your good! If health is part of your good, have a clear idea of how sweet and joyous health will feel. Name it as your good. When you have a clear idea of your good, it will come and settle upon you. It will manifest itself through you. It can burst forth in your life by the little sounds in your system. Jesus said, "The meek shall inherit the earth" (Matthew 5:5). Let this be in your mouth also. Be definite when you give this statement of good, which is the statement of your being. Expect to see it work quickly in your life. Truth is not slow. Truth is quick. Truth it now! Second Corinthians 6:2 says, "For he saith, I have heard thee in a time accepted, and in the day of salvation have I succored thee: behold, now is the accepted time; behold, now is the day of salvation."

Jesus said, "Now is the accepted time." Truth does not have to make things new for you. In truth, everything has been made new since the beginning. All truth is waiting for you to declare your good. Declaring continuously what we have felt intuitively is the first step toward demonstration, manifestation, and satisfaction. You have to declare your truth. Do not be afraid. Do not let outside circumstances stop you from declaring your truth. Know that God is your source and that he is the infinite source. Any time you start limiting God, know that it is your humanness, not your truth that is limiting you. Declare your truth, and it will unfold in your life.

Continually declare, "The good that I am seeking is my God." Now, that good could be anything. It could be prosperity. It could be health. It could be joy. It could be a loving relationship. If you mix any kind of disease with your truth, know that it is not of God. Any time doubt tries to creep in, go back to the truth that God has deposited in your heart and declare it. Keep your eyes on it. Hold steadfast to it. God put your truth in you because he has previously decreed that you will have it. It is available to you. It is yours. Your Father wants to give you the kingdom! As Jesus says, "Fear not, little flock; for it is your Father's good pleasure to give you the kingdom" (Luke 12:32).

AFFIRMATION

Now declare this affirmation of your good and expect God to deliver:

"The good I am seeking is my God. God is my life. The good I am seeking is my health. God is my health. The good I am seeking is my strength. God is my strength. The good I am seeking is my support. God is my support. The good I am seeking is my defense. God is my defense. Life is God. Truth is God. Love is God. Substance is God. God is intelligence, omnipresence, omnipotence, and omniscience. God is life omnipresent, omnipotent, and omniscient. God is truth omnipresent, omnipotent, and omniscient. God is love omnipresent, omnipotent, and omniscient. God is spirit omnipresent, omnipotent, and omniscient. God is truth."

5

Why are You Here?

"But there is a God in heaven (and heaven is within you) who reveals secrets, and He has made known to King Nebuchadnezzar what will be in the latter days. Your dream and the vision of your head upon your bed were these."
(Daniel 2:28)

Most of us have a job and a hobby. We often dream of retirement because it will allow us to concentrate on our hobby. We use our vacation and spare time to work on our hobbies. Why are we here? One of the reasons we are on earth is to manifest our passions. Many of us transcend without discovering our true passions. So what is passion? And how do we discover our passions? Our passions are that special something that we love doing and would do regardless of money, time, or any other obstacle. Thus, hobbies are oftentimes our true passions. When we operate from our passions, we operate with zeal, excitement, and eagerness. We never get tired or lack enthusiasm. Your passion—that gift—is your love; it is a gift from your Father. One of the reasons you are here is the development of your passion.

Developing your passion requires action. Passion is the seed that you must sow to reap prosperity such as money, property, business, and ownership. However, prior to sowing, what does the wise farmer do? He prepares the soil; he makes it fruitful by adding compost, fertilizer, nitrogen, and manure, and by letting the land rest and lie fallow for a season. He does all these things to ensure that the ground will yield what he intends to plant. This is the same process you must undergo as you work to retake control of your own life's crop and make it sustainable in good times and hard.

Reflect on the amendments the farmer adds to his soil. An amendment is something that promotes change. It does not bring about the change on its own, but it sets the stage for it and makes the ground ready for the planting of innovative ideas and a new prospect. With the system of God as your foundation, you must make the soil fruitful and add your own amendments so profitable change will come into your life. When times are hard and you cannot see your way to immediate hope, fertilize the soil! Eventually, new increase will appear, but only if you have prepared your position. The scriptures tell us that in the beginning was the word, and the word was God. Your beginning is your relationships, your ideas, your habits, your mind, your health, your practices, your knowledge, your biases, and your connection with God. Those are the seeds of your prosperity in the physical world! When harvest time comes, what you reap will be a direct consequence of how well you have made your beginning fertile while times were hard.

This, in fact, is the purpose of the cycles and seasons of life: to allow us the space and time to tend to the garden of our beginnings. We reexamine and remake ourselves the most in times of struggle and crisis. A man who has been obese all his life may get serious about exercise and diet after he has a heart attack. This is because we live in the moment, and complacency deceives us into thinking that we can remain static and healthy. God did not design a static universe. He designed everything to move, change, and evolve, including us. So when you lose your job, have no money, or are faced with economic uncertainty, these are times to rejoice! These are the seasons when we grow and evolve into new forms—something we will never do while we are secure and self-satisfied.

Our Passion Gives Us Purpose

God reveals his secrets. That internal conversation must operate from the desire fulfilled. In essence, we must declare the end from the beginning as the end dictates the beginning. "Declaring the end from the beginning, and from ancient times the things that are not yet done, saying, My counsel shall stand, and I will do all my pleasure" (Isaiah 46:10).

That inner speech is each of our individual passions. It is our inner conversations and our passions that drive us toward our future. Our passions cause us to excel at the very thing we are working on. Passion pushes us to greater heights. We always want to do more and to do better. Our passions give us purpose. We cannot have a passion without a purpose. However, our passions must give way to our purposes. As Psalm 42:1 says, "As the deer pants for the water brooks, so pants my soul for you, O God." Although we operate in our passions, we must remember that humility before God is one of our noblest attributes.

Humbling ourselves before God shows that we are not the fountain of our welfare or the makers of our lives. We are the recipients of God's generosity and should conduct ourselves as such. However, when things are going well, humility seems to elude many of us. At the same time, working in your passion means you are operating in the will of the Father. When you are enlightened and use your knowledge of spirit to shape your own character, you become an individual who looks at improvements. You move toward your fortunes with gratitude and humility. You are then able to leverage those improvements to lift your own situation and the situations of those around you. When we cultivate discipline and hard work at all times, even before prosperity has found us, we have the tools to multiply that fortune ten or a hundred times over. We do this by the means of industry, innovation, and persistence.

We also see in Proverbs 22:4 that the reward of humility and the fear of the Lord are riches, honor, and life. The self-inflated personality of the wealthy ignores the truth of this scripture and hopes that wealth and riches can continue even when God turns off the stream of plenty. However, this view is demonstrably false. In fact, the root cause of our recent economic crisis is haughtiness. There is nothing wrong with contentment in one's accomplishments, as long as you remember that everything you achieve is by the grace of God's system and your divine mind.

God Has Written On Our Heart
The verb *pant* is expressive of a spiritual thirst. That thirst—that passionate direction—will drive us to fulfill our accomplishments. Genuine self-interest means knowing our purpose. In essence, it means being in agreement with the longings God has written on our hearts. It also means pursuing the good that is our existence. We moreover have a combined purpose, which

is to reawaken Christlike values and steer toward the kingdom of God.

Why are we here? We know that God created us in his image and likeness. Thus we are spirit, and our bodies are temples of the Holy Ghost. If we are spirit created in the image and likeness of God, our function on this planet has to be very significant. Could our purpose be to express the purpose of the Spirit of God? Did God put us here to manifest his plan? Could this be the very purpose for our creation? However, the materialization of prosperity is a direct outcome of the state of mind that you sustain! A beneficial outlook produces favorable results; a fearful mind attracts objects of fear into your path.

In essence, we can accomplish whatever we put our minds to. It is a humbling and thrilling concept to think that we are here to carry out the Father's will. However, this idea poses another question: How do we know the Father's will for each of us? And how do we express the purpose of spirit on this planet? Philippians 3:13–14 says, "In contrast, one thing I do not count myself to have apprehended; however, one thing I do, forgetting those things which are behind and reaching forward to those things which are ahead, I press toward the goal for the prize of the upward call of God in Christ Jesus." When you're operating in the Father's will, you operate in great humility. You know you are humble when you are quick to attribute accomplishments to those around you and to God. You realize that you must be a worthy recipient of God's generosity and that you must help others along the way.

Humbleness also means that you are not set in your ways. You are flexible and willing to change for the better. You recognize that your circumstances are just a season in life. When you are not emotionally attached to your current situation, you can transform yourself to better serve others and share the message of enlightenment. In a perfect example, you are flowing with gratitude.

For most of us, abundance ebbs and flows and life comes with good times but also with tragedy. If you are humble, you take nothing for granted because you know that what has come to you could leave just as quickly.

We Are Always Creating

It is necessary to have an aim in life. We are always in a state of being and becoming. Without an aim, we merely drift through life. As a matter of fact, if we are not growing and becoming, we are dying. In short, we are always in a creating mode because that is the will of the Father. We are never the same one day to the next. John 10:10 states, "I have come that they may have life, and that they may have it more abundantly." Copious life includes salvation, nourishment, healing, and much more. Through the power of our minds, we can have the plentiful lives Christ promises us.

Abundance often disguises itself as our passions (that special something we love to do). We must prepare to receive this abundance. If we are serious about receiving abundance, then we must first gradually eliminate all unnecessary thoughts, desires, and habits from our lives. We must also walk in a state of awareness of the God who dwells within us. Walking in a state of awareness means that God will guide us from inside ourselves. It also denotes being still and allowing the Spirit to channel from within. We are the light of the world, and by this light we manifest the thoughts that we sanction. Remember! "All things that are exposed are made apparent by the light, for whatever makes evident is light" (Ephesians 5:13).

We Are Never Trapped

As humans, we are in a continuous state of being and becoming. We need to pause and feel joy and freedom in the fact that we are continually changing day by day. We are never trapped or stuck in any situation, regardless of how the circumstances may seem. Change is always there, waiting for us to make the decision. The fact that we are in a constant mode of change shows us why we are here. We are creators. We are creating the world. The creativeness in us comes from our creator. The power within us guides this creativity. We are cocreators with our Father. John 15:4 states, "Abide in me, and I in you, as the branch cannot bear fruit of itself." For the branch to produce more fruit, it must abide, which means to dwell, to stay, to settle in, and to sink deeper within.

6

WHAT ARE YOU SEEING?

"Seeing ye have purified your souls in obeying the truth through the Spirit unto unfeigned love of the brethren, see that ye love one another with a pure heart fervently."
(1 PETER 1:22)

WHAT ARE YOU seeing? What we see reflects what we are thinking, and we are what we think. Since we are what we think, and what we see affects our thinking, how does one control what one sees? First, it is essential to comprehend that everyone sees through their mind and not their eyes. Therefore, thoughts affect the way we see. Furthermore, what we believe determines what we see. This statement is true for all of us. Two people can look at the same object and see two very different things. Could I tell you that we see what we believed? Our beliefs are a powerful influence in our lives as we filter everything through our belief systems. They are also difficult to change through typical rules of logic or rational thinking.

There is a story about a group of refrigerator repair men who were working late on a Friday afternoon. The men were all working on large industrial walk-in refrigerators. After the men finished their work, they left for the weekend. One man was so engrossed in what he was doing that he forgot to check the time. When he was finished, he went to open the door, but it was locked from the outside. On returning to work on Monday, his colleagues found him frozen to death. The mystery, however, was that the refrigerators were not plugged in. The man saw in his mind that the refrigerator was working and functioning, and so he froze to death.

Our Mental Picture
It is imperative to grasp this concept, as it also relates to how we name things. We often name or call things according to the circumstances that exist at the time. Being conscious of how our thoughts are affected will help to clarify our mental picture. Having a clear vision allows one the opportunity to name things accurately. We name a thing based on our considerations about it at the particular time. Furthermore, how we name a thing reflects how we interact with that entity. Genesis 2:19 tells us that God "brought them unto Adam to see what he would call them; and whatsoever Adam called every living creature, that was the name thereof."

This is God delegating authority to man, since the act of naming the animals shows lordship or dominion. The scripture is telling us we have the ability, the power, and the dominion to name our situations. It is vital that we feel love before we name a thing, a situation, circumstances, and so on. God did not change the names Adam gave to every living creature. Whatever we call it is what it becomes to us.

Emotional Attachment

God will not change the way we choose to see. We have a tendency to name things based on our past experience and emotional attachment. Very often we allow our emotions to control our thoughts and ultimately our sight. How often do we formulate a view based on someone else's impression? How often have we allowed ourselves to absorb the emotions of others, thereby letting their energy infiltrate our mind, thoughts, and consciousness?

This all speaks to the importance of seeing with one's inner eye. Sight is based on knowledge of the thing. From birth, we have been bombarded with images of objects. In this world of mass communication, we are further saturated with images of scarcity and devastation. All this helps to form our thoughts and, consequently, what we think and see. Our thoughts then form who we are. Sometimes it may be necessary to correct old impressions. We may have to rename some of our experiences in order to move forward and avoid repeating them.

Old experiences often come back to alter your present. If we do not rename them, we tend to live in the past. And if that past was negative, it will impact negatively our present and who we are.

The Mental Image

Mental images are formed when something significant happens in our life. As new, similar experiences occur, we tend to react according to the conceptual image stored in our minds. Correcting old impressions is not an easy fix. It takes time, for one must be continually renewing one's mind and thoughts. First, awareness of the past hurt must be recognized in order to be renamed. If these thoughts, impressions, and mental images of yesteryear are not corrected, they can often stop one's growth. In essence, we will be trapped in the past like a car tire struck in the mud, spinning and getting nowhere. Romans 12:2 puts it this way: "And be not conformed to this world: nevertheless, be ye transformed by the renewing of your mind that ye may prove what is good, and acceptable, and perfect, will of God."

"Be not conformed" means to stop conforming. You are to resist the present-day thinking, value systems, and conduct of this world. We each want the very best life has to offer. As a result, we work hard with all our capacities in order to succeed. However, our best efforts can be wasted if we allow negative thoughts from the past to intrude into our present. The problem of a lack of success, however, lies in one's thought process. The past will emerge to influence our present if it is not reversed. Past images, if not cleaned up and renamed, could be blocking growth. It could also block or alter the image of your true self.

I Deemed Myself as Having a Weight Problem

It is difficult not to be affected by surroundings, even with the knowledge that we see with our mind's eye. For example, in the world's view and in my own mind, I thought I had a weight problem. Even when I weighed ninety-nine pounds, I still felt overweight. I had to go within and conduct a self-examination to determine where I picked up that concept. It was revealed to me that for many years as a child, I was told that I would be fat like my aunt. This thought became embedded in my consciousness and tormented me for a very long time. However, recognizing the source of the torment means I can now forgive and can thereby alter my past and present.

Being bombarded with negative images and poverty every day would have an impact on anyone's thoughts. It's like throwing mud on a wall. While most of it might fall off, some will stick. How do we prevent our perception of present negative circumstances from altering and eventually damaging our thoughts? This is done by the renewal of one's mind as often as necessary. Second Corinthians 4:16 says, "For which cause we faint not; save for though our outward man perishes, yet the inward man is renewed day by day."

Do this ten times a day if that is what it takes. You are what you think. What are you thinking? Remember, what you do not prepare for could determine where you end up. You must have the right foundation so new circumstances do not throw you off track. As you correct and continue on your path, remember you serve one master. Your life is valuable. However, without purpose, you are not going anywhere. You shall remain stagnant, slowing dying, instead of progressing.

Actions Form Patterns

Your steps or actions are primary to what you are, in much the same way as particles are basic units or material. These actions form patterns, and these patterns tell a story. Your actions tell a narrative about you. To put it differently, all the energy and different aspects that exercise their authority in life and in the world are represented at the point of the individual act. These then divulge their distinctive function at your individual level. Another example is the way an individual cell functions within an organ and then as part of your body.

Ralph's Speeding Ticket: When you start to distinguish how your actions are repeated, you can benefit from your assessments of them. For example, you can learn to recognize when to take or not take actions based on a previous occurrence of the same performance. That is, if you recognize a negative pattern, you can divert its reoccurrence in the future. Here is an experience from real life. My husband, Ralph, would receive a speeding ticket every year around the time of his birthday. This pattern went on for years. He would receive the ticket and then exclaim, "Oh, this is my yearly ticket!" without observing the pattern. However, once he recognized the pattern, he was able to change his thought process so that he no longer anticipated receiving a ticket. This resulted in no further speeding tickets at all.

Ralph first had to notice the frequency, then assume the traffic ticket was likely to be repeated (based on the pattern), and then take precautions to prevent reoccurrence when his next birthday came around. Now, as a result of perceiving the pattern, Ralph has altered the course of his life.

7

WE ARE ALWAYS EVOLVING

"For as he thinketh in his heart, so is he: Eat and drink, saith he to thee; but his heart is not with thee."
(PROVERBS 23:7)

YOU ARE THE sum total of your thoughts. Human thoughts travel 168 thousand miles per second, which is 930 thousand times faster than the sound of our voices. We do not articulate most of our thoughts, and yet they determine what we are and what we are becoming. We may not voice a particular thought, but the mere fact that we think it means that it will affect our lives. We may think that we can let our minds wander off without it having any negative impact on our bodies. After all, they are just our thoughts. They are not hurting anyone. Well, nothing could be further from reality! Negative thinking is very damaging. It is damaging to our bodies, our minds, and our manifestations.

This section addresses our thoughts as they speak to our identities. Genesis 6:5 states: "And God saw that the wickedness of man was great in the earth, and that every imagination of the thought of his heart was only evil continually." However, when you become one with your assignment and submit to it, you allow God to be God and to demonstrate his glory through you to its fullest extent. First Corinthians 12:1 says, "Now concerning spiritual gifts, brethren, I would not have you ignorant."

Wisdom comes through forgiveness. If you can change your attitude toward anyone you can forgive them. To forgive is also to forget. When Job turned from himself and prayed for his friends, his own captivity was lifted. "And the Lord turned the captivity of Job, when he prayed for his friends: also the Lord gave Job twice as much as he had before" (Job 42:10). How did Job do it? You can do it with your own thoughts. It would cost you nothing right now to lift up your fellow man. See them as God sees them: perfect and whole in every way. Do it without looking for any earthly rewards.

Everything Begins with Thought
The New Testament further explains the importance of thoughts and unmistakably tells us what defiles a person. Matthew 15:19 explains what thoughts can produce: "For out of the heart proceed evil thoughts, murders, adulteries, fornications, thefts, false witness, and blasphemies." This verse shows us what our thoughts are capable of producing and is telling us that we must learn to control our thoughts.

Everything begins with a thought. The conditions you are facing right now materialized from your thoughts. Every so-called problem we encounter first originated from our thoughts. Even wicked schemes flow from immoral thoughts. Furthermore, "blasphemies" in Matthew 15:19 refers not only to blasphemy in the narrow, modern sense of the word, but also to criticism or libel of others. It does not end there. Proverbs 18:21 puts it this way: "Death and life are in the power of the tongue." However, what do you believe? It doesn't matter what you say but what you believe.

As Jesus says, "Let not your heart be troubled: ye believe in God, believe also in me" (John 14:1). The one speaking is God, the Jesus in you.

Here is a test I would like you to conduct. When you say you believe in God, and an image of something or someone outside of yourself emerges in your mind, you are in the world and not in the spirit. "God is a Spirit: and they that worship him must worship him in spirit and in truth" (John 4:24).

The world cannot answer your prayers. Remember, you are the temple of the living God, and the Spirit of God dwells within you.

You Are the Compilation of Your Thoughts

You are the compilation of all your thoughts. In essence, you are what you think. You are what you pay mind to. You don't have to be clairvoyant to know what is on a person's mind. You only have to look at the person's surroundings to get a window into his or her mind. Whatever you pay mind to will manifest in your life. Observing a person's habits and friends can paint a clear picture of his or her identity. My mentor puts it this way: "Your friends are your prophecy." They tell you where you are heading. The Bible also outlines clearly what the content of your thoughts should be. Philippians 4:8 puts it this way: "Finally, brethren, whatever things are true, whatsoever things are just; whatever things are pure, whatsoever things are lovely, whatsoever things are of a good report; if there be any virtue, and if there be any praise, think about these things."

There is a story about a woman who traveled to New York for a very important business meeting with some clients. After spending her whole day shopping, she was extremely tired. She had a one-hour train ride to her hotel. She boarded the train with her parcels and decided that she was going to sleep for that one hour so that by the time she reached the hotel, she would be rested. All she would have to do was take a shower and get ready for her meeting.

She boarded the train and found her seat. Opposite her sat a man and his three children. The children were very loud and disruptive. She couldn't sleep at all. She looked at the man, and he seemed oblivious to the children's behavior. He was in a world of his own and appeared not be concerned by their actions. The woman went over to the man and asked, "Are these your children?"

The man responded, "Yes."

"What is the matter with you?" she asked. "Can't you see that they're misbehaving?"

The man replied, "Right now we're heading home from the hospital where they found out that their mother had just died, and I guess they don't know how to deal with it yet."

Shocked by the man's story, the woman apologized and went back to her seat. The children continued playing and making noise, but somehow the woman could now sleep.

When you know who your master is, outside circumstances should not bother you. Do not try to fix external situations; do not try to control them. You just have to know who you are serving and where you are going. If you can keep your eyes on God, whatever happens around you will not deter you from your goal. Outside events will just roll off your back. They will have no emotional effect on you. When you submit to God within you, everything outside you will be in divine order.

The book of Numbers teaches us that the world views us the way we view ourselves:

> And Caleb stilled the people before Moses, and said, Let us go up at once, and possess it; for we are well able to overcome it. Nevertheless, the men who went up with him said, we be not able to go up against the people; for they are stronger than we. And they brought up an evil report of the land which they had searched unto the children of Israel, saying, The land, through which we have gone to search it, is a land that eateth up the inhabitants thereof; and all the people that we saw in it are men of a great stature. And there we saw the giants, the sons of Anak, which come of the giants: and we were in our own sight as grasshoppers, and so we were in their sight. (Numbers 13:30–33)

Every Action Has a Preceding Thought
The scriptures say that to keep God's peace, people must occupy their minds with the right things and busy themselves with the right activities. The Bible is saying that words and thoughts have power, and thoughts determine what manifests in this earthly realm. The Bible offers these words of caution because all actions are the result of thoughts. Whatever you are doing right now first appeared as a thought in your mind, whether you were aware of the thought or not. Every action has a preceding thought. Nothing occurs unless it first appeared as a thought in the mind.

We can no longer afford the luxury of unorganized thoughts. We must practice correct thinking.

When we practice correct thinking, we attract the right actions and obtain the right results. These truths not only alert us to pay attention to our thoughts, but also place a tremendous burden on us to accept responsibility for our present circumstances. This is a tall order because it is very easy to blame something or someone else for your present predicament. However, do not panic; the same way you thought yourself into your dilemma, you can think yourself out of it.

Thoughts Are Seeds We Plant
Who are you? You are your thoughts, and your thoughts are you. You are what you think all day long. In essence, you are the sum total of your thoughts. It is extremely important to be in command of your thoughts and not to allow the mind to drift into unconstructive thoughts. Like attracts like! As a result, you will manifest whatever is in your thoughts.

A story from my youth comes to mind. A soccer club from a major city was visiting our city for the first time. One night, a group of us took the players out for dinner at one of my favorite restaurants. The restaurant was in an area of town that I frequented. I felt safe there and had never observed any illicit activities. However, minutes after arriving at the restaurant, a member of the visiting soccer team was able to purchase prohibited pharmaceuticals on the street. This made an impression on me because I had never observed such activities in that part of town.

This story illustrates the idea that you will find what you seek. Galatians 6:7 puts it this way: "Whatsoever a man soweth, that he also reaps." The seeking first occurs in the mind. In essence, thoughts are seeds that we plant in our minds.

Communicating Your Thoughts

There is a power in the universe that honors our faith in it; there is a law in the universe that exacts down to the smallest farthing. We all wish to feel the power behind everything good. Intuitively, we sense that every man, in his native state, is some part of the manifestation of this eternal principle. It has been written that the truth shall make us free (John 8:32), provided that we know the truth, and we note that the evolution of mankind's consciousness brings with it the acquisition of new powers and higher possibilities. As Romans 13:1 says, "Let every soul be subject unto the higher powers. For there is no power but of God: the powers that be are ordained of God."

We access this power through our thoughts about ourselves, and these thoughts expand out into the world. In essence, we communicate with our thoughts by just thinking them. If your thoughts do not match your spoken words, you may deceive others for a time; however, they will always have an uneasy feeling about you. In other words, we can deceive others with our words but not with our thoughts. This nonverbal communication is very powerful. Consequently, it is wise to be aware that you are communicating the thoughts that are prevailing in your head. Your thoughts are an expression of who you are. Essentially, your thoughts are you. Proverbs 23:7 puts it this way: "For as he thinketh in his heart, so is he."

For as He Thinks, So Is He

This is also saying that whatever you sow in your mind, your heart will bear as fruit. In essence, your thoughts will manifest as who you are. What thoughts you deposit in your mind will grow. Your thoughts are shaping you into the person you are becoming. We are always evolving, and our thoughts are the catalyst for this process. Your thoughts form you, and you form your thoughts. So it makes sense that if you are the sum total of your thoughts, then you have the ability to become whatever you want.

It is well established scientifically that the mind moves the body. Our thought processes control the movement of our bodies. Your thoughts also affect how you see. As we conclude this chapter, let us reflect on a few verses from 1 Corinthians:

> For as the body is one, and hath many members, and all the members of that one body, being many, are one body: so also is Christ. For by one Spirit are we all baptized into one body, whether we be Jews or Gentiles, whether we be bond or free; and have been all made to drink into one Spirit. For the body is not one member, but many. (1 Corinthians 12:12–14)

8

The Mind is the Battleground

"But God came to Abimelech in a dream by night, and said to him, Behold, thou art but a dead man, for the woman which thou hast taken; for she is a man's wife. But Abimelech had not come near her."
(Genesis 20:3–4)

WHO ARE YOU? Are you a product of your past experiences? How strongly do your parents influence your current thoughts? Do past incidents and circumstances contribute to your present philosophy and ideology? Do your parents, grandparents, teachers, and other people affect the decisions you make today? These are all factors that can impact your life. If these people or past experiences were negative, you could find yourself in a rut. People in this situation continually make the same mistakes and attract the wrong people into their lives. Depending on the extent of the negative experiences, past teachings can even affect our present relationships! This chapter addresses those tapes that keep playing in your mind—those tapes that you would like to turn off but don't quite know how.

A Product of Our Past

We are all products of our pasts. Our pasts helped shape us into the people we are today. Whether or not we want to admit it, the dominant people in our lives significantly impact who we become as individuals. While they may have a positive influence, a negative impact can also be an imprisonment. However, we don't have to let old and negative beliefs keep us captive because we are always being and becoming. We can always change our current circumstances through our thought processes. We all want to capture the best from our past experiences.

However, the pain and hurt of past experiences tend to dominate our thoughts. The key is to ensure that those thoughts do not rob us of our present. To accomplish this, we must first learn to forgive. "Father, forgive them" was Jesus's cry on the cross. What cross are you carrying that you cannot forgive? To forgive is also to forget. As humans, we can forgive but not forget. It doesn't really matter how often you miss the mark and become frustrated. We must practice the art of forgiveness and go through life forgiving others. Forgive every being on this planet, for you are not meant to condemn them. Instead, you should lift them up out of that state. If people displease you, it is your responsibility to lift them out of that state and bring them to a state that is pleasing to you. You must do this in divine order without causing harm to anyone.

The Mind Is a Battleground

The mind is a battleground. Change must begin in our minds. Change occurs within. The mind is also our dwelling place. It is where we live all day long. It is our habitation, and in our habitation, we tend to adopt certain lifestyles, routines, traditions, rituals, and customs. Those traditions and customs all come from our thoughts. They reflect who we are and who we are becoming. Thoughts are expressed as routines, customs, and habits. To become the people we think we are, we must clean up our habitations. This cleaning process also addresses those lifestyles, routines, traditions, rituals, and customs that negatively impact our present-day lives. Our dwelling place must be safe and free from worry and fear. It must be a place of security for us. It must be the most high place where one could dwell. Psalm 91:1 puts it this way: "He that dwelled in the secret place of the most high shall abide under the shadow of the Almighty."

The key word to describe this psalm is "refuge," a place of safety. One's inward expression reflects one's outward expression. The mind can acquire a state of calm, peace, and tranquility. Other scriptures also speak about a pleasant rest in one's mind. For example, Psalm 23:2–4 states:

> He maketh me to lie down in green pastures: he leadeth me beside the still waters. He restoreth my soul: he leadeth me in the paths of righteous for his name's sake. Yea though I walk through the valley of the shadow of death, I will fear no evil: for thou art with me, thy rod and thy staff they comfort me.

The Mind Is Its Own Place

This psalm tells us that God is our protector and provider in life. God our protector dwells in us. The mind is the beginning point of everything you do. In essence, if you can gain control of your mind, you can gain control of your external circumstances. The mind is its own place, and of itself it can make a heaven of hell or a hell of heaven. In other words, our minds are our own God or our own devil. It is all up to you and how you want to name it. This is an oversimplification, of course, as spiritual laws and systems are also at work. Nonetheless, when you harbor negative or harmful thoughts, you are, in effect, making a hell of your present heaven.

For example, I had what the world calls dyslexia, and for many years, in spite of my accomplishments, I thought that I was inadequate and not quite as intelligent as my colleagues. Through the teachings of the master prophet, I came to know who I am. I also know that I am blessed with superb wisdom and intelligence. Understand this: Your mind has the ability to put away thoughts that are not profitable for you.

Live in the Now
Guilt, fear, and regrets can all wreak havoc on your thoughts and influence your emotions. Nevertheless, to overcome the past, it is necessary to forgive. Forgiveness of oneself and of others is absolutely necessary in becoming the person you wish to be. Pain from past experiences often lingers and influences the present, but it does not have to. Trying to become something from the past or attempting to relive the past will negatively affect your present. You can move forward only when you stop living in the past. You must get out of both the past and the future and live in the now. We all have the ability to change and develop. This requires letting go of those painful and negative experiences from the past. It also means putting an end to "pity parties" and feeling sorry for yourself.

The Mind Is a Powerful Tool
The mind is a powerful tool. If we dwell on something long enough, it will manifest. If your mind is having a "pity party," you will become disheartened. For example, there are people in Europe who manifested the nail marks of the crucified Jesus

Christ on their bodies. Anyone can experience the same result if they spend enough time dwelling emotionally on the Passion.

This concept is applicable to everyone's thought processes. Any individual can manifest any result he desires on his body if he focuses his thoughts and feelings on it. You must convert what you take into your mind into manifestation on the body, since the mind and the body are one. We are what we imagine all day long. Individuals often make themselves sick through their thoughts. We are under the influence of our own negative thoughts and deeds; we are under no other influences. We just love to blame some outside force for our circumstances and the people we become because of those circumstances.

The reality, however, for the majority of the time is that we are the products of our own follies and are responsible for the unwise conduct that manifests from our unwise thoughts. We often hear the phrase "sins of the fathers" used to explain someone's negative behavior. What does it mean? We love to blame our misfortunes, woes, shortcomings, bad habits, and other deeds of destruction on the sins of our forefathers. Although I can't address what that means in a spiritual context, I do recognize that right thinking can fix most of our experiences. Hosea 4:6 puts it this way: "My people are destroyed for lack of knowledge."

Man's Problem Is "Lack of Knowledge"
Here the scripture is telling us that the foundation of man's problem is "lack of knowledge." It does not stem from a lack of information, but rather from rejection of information. Lack of knowledge or rejection of knowledge allows us to form certain habits. We are our habits, and our habits reflect who we are. Our habits are where we live. They are what we know and are comfortable with, whether it is negative or not. It is this comfort

with old habits that we must change. We have all heard people complain about one thing or another; however, if we make a suggestion to help, the complainers have a million and one reasons why the suggestion would not work. The truth is that they are comfortable with their situations and have no intention of changing despite their complaints.

The Old Must Die to Birth the New
To be the people we think we are, we must correct our thinking. It is possible to change your habits and, as a result, your habitation. If you would like to break a habit, do something different from the habit for thirty days. For example, if you want to stop taking your tea with sugar, take your tea without sugar for thirty days. At the end of that thirty-day period, you will no longer crave sugar in your tea and you will be well on your way to controlling that habit.

We can change habits. This rule illustrates the principle that the old must die to birth the new. The scriptures put it this way in Matthew 9:17: "Neither do men put new wine into old bottles: else the bottles break, and the wine runneth out, and the bottles perish: but they put new wine into new bottles, and both are preserved."

The principle expressed here is that the Lord Jesus Christ has come to bring in a whole new dispensation that cannot fit into the old Jewish economy. This is the same standard you are trying to convey. You are bringing in a new habit that cannot fit into the old way. As a result, the old habit must die for the new replacement to survive. That death could occur over the thirty-day period. Knowing and then acting on this principle gives you power over the decisions you make. By changing how you think or view a situation, you can change your negative habits, routines, practices, behaviors, and lifestyle for healthier ones.

Jesus said, "Think not that I have come to abolish the law and the prophets. I am come not to abolish them but to fulfill them" (Matthew 5:17). According to a speech by Neville from a publication titled *The Neville Reader*, imagination is the basis of all that exists. You may commune with what you think is someone other than yourself. However, because there are billions of people in the world and only one God, you might wonder if he hears you. Nevertheless, if you identify God with your own wonderful human imagination, you have no doubt in your mind that he hears you.

9

How to Retain Information

"And I will remember my covenant, which is between me and you and every living creature of all flesh; and the waters shall no more become a flood to destroy all flesh."
(Genesis 9:15)

As we examine who we are and why we are here, we may discover that we have a habit or two to transform. To become the people we know we are in Christ, some changes must occur. Therefore, we must unlearn certain things and replace them with new and exciting patterns and behaviors that will help us become our true selves. How do we learn these new behaviors? Let's face it; all the information discussed in the book means nothing unless you take action and put it into practice. Therefore, the main objective of this chapter is to explore the principles of adult learning and apply them during our quest for knowledge. Understanding how we learn as adults will help us recognize our habits before they turn into patterns. This chapter also shares some techniques for implementing planned behavior and patterns that will lead to positive outcomes. As Romans 12:2 says, "But be ye transformed by the renewing of your mind, that ye may prove what is good, and acceptable, and perfect, will of God."

Learning Occurs First from Within

Romans 12:2 tells us that change must first occur in the mind before we can make it happen in our day-to-day experiences. Adult learning occurs within us as a continual process throughout our lives, and learning also occurs at different speeds for each of us. So what is learning? Learning is a gaining of knowledge.

Knowledge can either benefit us or harm us. We are bombarded with information every day. We retain some of it and leave the rest behind. So what happens that causes us to retain certain information? First, it is important for us to recognize what form of learning will help us remember pertinent information most effectively. To accomplish this, let's look at the average retention rate after twenty-four hours of exposure to new data and how this can help us become that person we know within. Mark 11:24 says, "Therefore, I say to you, whatever things you ask when you pray, believe that you receive them, and you will have them." Notice that Jesus says we must simply believe that we will receive what we've asked for; we must believe in our inner strength as we press forward.

How to Retain Information

We know that our brains take in all information through our representational systems (our five senses). In NLP, those five senses are called:
- Visual
- Auditory

- Kinesthetic
- Olfactory
- Gustatory

Not everyone receives information in the same way. For example, some of us learn better by visual means and others by auditory means. Regardless of which sense we use best, we retain a limited amount of information based on how the information is presented. This chapter will help you identify the best method to use when trying to retain information.

Lectures: Five Percent Retention
In our search to comprehend who we are, we may attend lectures on self-realization. We may receive very good information, but research tells us that we will retain only 5 percent of the information we receive from lectures. Attending one lecture on a subject will not change a well-developed habit.

Reading: Ten Percent Retention
Next, we may obtain several books on various subjects that will enlighten us and help us along our path. But to implement information we gain from books, we must first retain the information. Reading allows us to retain just 10 percent of what we comprehend. The use of lectures plus reading will strengthen our average retention rates. Thus, we will retain more when we read and listen to a lecture. In addition, to guard our minds and thoughts, we must pay attention to our listening and reading materials. Joshua 24:15 says, "Choose for yourselves this day whom you will serve." The scriptures are telling us to take a stand. As leaders, we must be willing to move ahead and commit to the truth regardless of other people's inclinations.

Sight and Audio: Twenty Percent Retention
Next on this spectrum are audiovisual materials. This medium uses both visual and audio communications to increase the average rate of retention to 20 percent. If you purchase an audiovisual tape on the subject matter you are trying to learn, the likelihood of retention is greater when combined with lecture and reading.

In conjunction with audiovisual material, we must pay attention to who is speaking in our ears. Negative people can damage all of our good works. Everyone has an opinion, and often others' opinions may not apply to us. Therefore, we must carefully guard our ears by discerning what we open ourselves and our minds to. As Philippians 4:8 says, "Whatever things are true, whatever things are noble, whatever things are just, whatever things are pure, whatever things are lovely, whatever things are of good report…meditate on these things."

Hands-On Approach: Thirty Percent Retention
The next principle by which adults learn is demonstration. A hands-on approach increases the probability for retention to 30 percent. Sometimes we may find ourselves in a profession that conflicts with our core values. In such cases, it is necessary to find another course of employment. Our profession is an extension of ourselves. We make choices in our jobs, and we can change those choices. It is foolhardy to think that our professional lives are distinct and separate from the people we are. We are what we do all day long. What we demonstrate, we will retain and become. In other words, if we do something long enough, we will become it. Our professions must therefore align with our core values. The scriptures put it this way: "Every kingdom divided against itself is brought to desolation; and every city or house divided against itself shall not stand" (Matthew 12:25).

Discussion Groups: Fifty Percent Retention

In a discussion group, we retain 50 percent of the information we learn. This is significant because it tells us that we cannot afford to demean anybody. If we do, we will retain the garbage we spit out. That garbage then becomes a part of us. We are our thoughts. This means we no longer have the luxury of partaking in negative gossip. We must learn to walk away from negative jokes, negative chatter, and negative thoughts as a whole. We are responsible for creating positive vibrations.

Practice: Seventy-Five Percent Retention

We have often heard the saying "practice what you preach." Practice is the next principle by which adults learn. Through practice, adults retain 75 percent of information. To guard our minds and thoughts, we must consider what we are practicing, for we will preserve it. Because we retain 75 percent of information when we practice, what we practice can be the very medium through which we form new habits. If we wish to adopt or learn something quickly, we should practice it.

Teaching: Ninety Percent Retention

The most significant way to retain information is to teach others. The immediate use of new information allows for 90 percent retention of information discussed. This is just awesome. To change old habits into new ones, we must teach the new habit to someone else. Teaching others puts us on the fast track to learning and retaining that information. If you want to learn something fast, teach it to someone else. By doing so, you will retain 90 percent of the information delivered. Understanding the average rate of retention is important. However, it is also important to be aware of some of the characteristics of adult learners.

Characteristics of Adult Learners

Adults tend to be problem oriented rather than subject oriented. Children are subject oriented because they lack adult experiences. However, by knowing this, we can conduct inner analyses, define the problem from within, and then implement a course of action to fix it. We are also inclined to be results oriented. Adults do not waste time. We tend to be focused and goal oriented. While our children are future oriented, we are focused on the results that we can achieve in the present.

By understanding this characteristic about ourselves, we will better recognize what is likely to make an impression on us and therefore be more discerning about the information we allow to take root. Also, adults are self-directed. The "teach me" behavior we often see in adults could stem from previous school experiences. Generally, adults are independent, self-directed learners. Understanding how we learn best can guide us to the best medium when gathering information for change. Unlike children, who tend to be more accepting, mature adults are less trusting and thus are often skeptical about receiving new information. This is a critical point to observe because it speaks to how we learn.

Understanding Our Skepticism

By understanding our skepticism about new information, we can then make a concerted effort to be more open to new ideas and concepts. Coupled with this is the suggestion that adults seek relevancy. The information we seek must apply to us in the present. Our children are often trained for an unclear future, but adults seek the exact information for the situation at hand. As fully developed, mature adults, we are internally rather than externally motivated to learn. A word of caution: Because the timing of our learning is related to our current issues or concerns, it is doubly important that we discern the correct information. We must take time to seek correct information to gain right thinking.

Accepting Responsibility

The majority of us accept responsibility for our own learning. This is yet another very important characteristic of how adults learn. If we do not find the correct method of delivery, we will not absorb the information, even if it is worthwhile. It is also important to find new and efficient ways of learning because we often have a limited amount of time. As adults, we must become active participants in the learning process. Anything other than active participation will result in us having to repeat the process several times.

Previous Knowledge Helps to Shape New

Adults actively create their knowledge. In other words, previous knowledge helps to shape new knowledge. We ascertain what we already know about a topic and then add to it. In essence, we activate prior knowledge and then personalize it and elaborate on what we already know. To determine the truth of who we are, some housekeeping may be necessary. We may have to unlearn some things and take in all new information. This is the most troublesome area we will encounter because the most important factor influencing us is what we have already learned. Adult education is designed to connect with what the learners already know. In this case, however, we must unlearn what we have already learned. We do not passively receive knowledge. As learners, we have to do something with the information; otherwise, it will not result in long-term retention.

Barriers Stem from Negative Thinking

As adults, we encounter many barriers to learning. These barriers stem from years of negative thinking that we have encountered throughout our lives. Some of the barriers we bring to learning may be low self-esteem, anxiety, fear, and insecurity. Fear and frustration are the most problematic because they often lead to helplessness that stunts our learning. We may also lack confidence and have low expectations of ourselves. On top of all that, we may also be struggling with domestic, financial, health, or personal worries while we are trying to learn.

Hopefully, by discovering who we are from the earlier chapters in the book, we will leave behind some of these barriers. We can view the barriers to learning as emotions. This is not as bad as it may appear because emotions are the key to learning. As we go through this whole process of unlearning and learning information, it is important to understand how our brain processes learn material. Our minds store information as a network of interconnected, related data. As a result, the processing of our thoughts leads to the activation of other related materials. We have already discussed the fact that the use of images can aid the learning process and retention better than verbal description.

Adults Are Problem Solvers
As adults, we are all about problem solving. We also like to focus on the big picture. We operate better from the end result. In other words, we know where we want to end up first, and then we set a course of action. However, attracting the end result through our thought process is quite another matter. As adults, we learn not primarily by receiving and copying information, but rather by assembling and reassembling our own mental formations of our worlds. In other words, understanding is largely internally constructed. Our brains are complex organs, and correct thinking requires deep processing. For correct thinking to become a part of who we are, we must obtain the information through self-directed learning. In essence, learning must be within our control. We must be able to accept responsibility for our own

learning. Remember, our judgments of our own abilities are central to our actions. Oftentimes, our self-judgments may not be accurate. In such instances, verbal persuasion from a credible source could prove valuable.

Chinese Proverb

Did you know that writing is the first form of manifestation? Writing also plays an important role in an adult learning principle called *penetrating observance*.

As you write, you reflect on what went before. That reflection on your past experiences allows you an opportunity to clean up any misunderstanding and help shape and correct actions that may affect future practice. Writing can provide the vehicle for these insightful observances. Finally, I would like to end with this Chinese proverb: "Tell me, and I'll forget; show me, and I may remember; involve me, and I'll understand."

Glossary of Terms

arche. Arche means "beginning rule" and is also often rendered "power." For example, Luke 20:20 says, "And they watched him, and sent forth spies, which feigned themselves just men, that might take hold of his words, so that they might deliver him into the power or authority of the governor."

body. With regard to living things, a body is an individual's integral physical material. In the views emerging from the mind-body dichotomy, the body is considered to be in opposition to a person's mind, soul, personality, and behavior, and is therefore unimportant. However, many modern philosophers maintain that the mind is not something separate from the body.

consubstantial. This means "regarded as the same in substance or essence" (as of the three persons of the Trinity). For example, Christ Jesus is coeternal and consubstantial with the Father and with the Holy Ghost.

cosmos. In its most general sense, a cosmos is an orderly or harmonious system. It originates from the Greek term κόσμος (meaning "order, orderly arrangement, ornaments") and is the antithetical concept to chaos. The word "cosmetics" originates from the same root.

creation. Creation is the belief that God brought the universe into existence (theology).

critical thinking. Critical thinking is the mental process of analyzing and evaluating statements or propositions that others have presented as true. It includes a process of reflecting on the specific meaning of statements, examining offered evidence, and reasoning to form a judgment.

critical thinkers. Critical thinkers can gather information from verbal or written expression, reflection, observation, experience, and reasoning. Critical thinking has its basis in intellectual criteria that go beyond subject-matter divisions and that include clarity, credibility, accuracy, precision, relevance, depth, breadth, logic, significance, and fairness.

dunamis. This Greek word means miracle-working power. The gospel of Christ is the power of God unto salvation; it is the miracle-working power that will bring deliverance.

divine economy. From the Greek word oikonomia (economy), this term literally means "management of a household" or "stewardship." It includes the elements and resources revealed by God as necessary for salvation through special revelation (i.e., the Old and New Testaments). The ultimate expression of this is the work of salvation by Jesus Christ on the cross. His sacrifice paid for our debts so that God would not see us as guilty for our sins. This economy is related to a transaction. God gives the means of salvation through Jesus's sacrifice. We accept it through faith and allegiance to him. It is an economy because it has resources, management, and accountability.

end times. Also called the end of days, this term usually refers to the eschatological ideas in the three Abrahamic religions

(Judaism, Christianity, and Islam). The end times are often (but not always) depicted as a time of tribulation that precedes the coming of a messianic figure.

ischus. This is a Greek word for power. It means ability, force, or strength. For example, 2 Thessalonians 1:9, speaking of those who do not know or obey the Lord, says, "[they] shall be punished with everlasting destruction from the presence of the Lord, and from glory of his power."

manifestations. In the mystical traditions, the manifestation, or being, is that which exists.

New Testament. The New Testament is a collection of twenty-seven books, produced by Christians, with Jesus as its central figure. The books were written primarily in Koine Greek in the early Christian period. Nearly all Christians recognize the New Testament (as listed below) as canonical scripture. These books can be grouped into the following categories:

The Gospels
- Synoptic Gospels
- Gospel According to Matthew (Mt)
- Gospel According to Mark (Mk)
- Gospel According to Luke (Lk)
- Gospel According to John (Jn)
- Acts of the Apostles (Ac; continues Luke)

Pauline Epistles
- Epistle to the Romans (Ro)
- First Epistle to the Corinthians (1 Co)
- Second Epistle to the Corinthians (2 Co)
- Epistle to the Galatians (Ga)
- Epistle to the Ephesians (Ep)
- Epistle to the Philippians (Pp)

- Epistle to the Colossians (Cl)
- First Epistle to the Thessalonians (1 Th)
- Second Epistle to the Thessalonians (2 Th)

Pastoral Epistles
- First Epistle to Timothy (1 Ti)
- Second Epistle to Timothy (2 Ti)
- Epistle to Titus (Tt)
- Epistle to Philemon (Pm)
- Epistle to the Hebrews (He)

General Epistles (also called Jewish Epistles)
- Epistle of James (Jm)
- First Epistle of Peter (1 Pe)
- Second Epistle of Peter (2 Pe)
- First Epistle of John (1 Jn)
- Second Epistle of John (2 Jn)
- Third Epistle of John (3 Jn)
- Epistle of Jude (Jd)
- Revelation (Re)

Old Testament. The Old Testament is the first section of the two-part Christian biblical canon. It includes the books of the Hebrew Bible as well as several deuterocanonical books. Its exact contents differ in the various Christian denominations.

the Protestant Old Testament. This version of the Old Testament is, for the most part, identical with the Hebrew Bible. The differences between the Hebrew Bible and the Protestant Old Testament are minor, dealing only with the arrangement and number of the books. For example, while the Hebrew Bible considers Kings to be a unified text, the Protestant Old Testament divides it into two books. Similarly, Ezra and Nehemiah are considered to be one book in the Hebrew Bible.

the difference between the Hebrew Bible and other versions of the Old Testament (such as the Samaritan Pentateuch, Syriac, Latin, Greek, and other canons) are greater. Many of these canons include books and even sections of books that the others do not.

There is abundant and reliable evidence that these books were written before the birth of Jesus of Nazareth, whose teaching and disciples' deeds and teachings are the subject of the subsequent writings of the Christians' New Testament.

the scriptures that Jesus used were according to Luke 24:44–49: "The law of Moses, and in the prophets, and in the psalms...the scriptures." According to most Bible scholars, the Old Testament was composed between the fifth century BC and the second century BC. However, parts of it, such as parts of the Torah and the Song of Deborah (Judges 5), probably date back much earlier.

omega point. This term was invented by French Jesuit Pierre Teilhard de Chardin to describe the maximum level of complexity in consciousness. He considered the omega point to be the direction toward which consciousness evolves.

omnipotence. This term means "all powerful." We recognize that we are dealing with omnipotence—all the power in the universe.

omniscience. This term means "all knowledge." There is not a problem in the universe to which omniscience does not know the answer. Omniscience has brought into existence everything that exists.

omnipresence. The term means "everywhere present." Omnipresence means that the infinite is equally present at all points in space; therefore the infinite can help a person living on the other side of the world just as easily as if he were in the same room.

treatment. A treatment consists of the formulation of a concept of perfection, accompanied by a conviction of its truth with the assurance that the creative law of mind, through omnipotence, omniscience, and omnipresence, invariably proceeds to translate it into form.

tensile strength. This is the maximum load that a material can support without fracture when being stretched, divided by the original cross-sectional area of the material.

triadocentric. This belief considers the divine life ad intra and ad extra, always beginning with the whole of the Trinity according to the patristic principle: Everything proceeds from the Father, through the Son in the Holy Spirit.

triadophoric. This term means "relating to the Trinity."

Trinity. In Christianity, the doctrine of the Trinity states that God is one being who exists, simultaneously and eternally, as a mutual indwelling of three persons: the Father, the Son (incarnate as Jesus of Nazareth), and the Holy Spirit. Since the fourth century, in both Eastern and Western Christianity, believers have stated this as "three persons in one God," all three of whom, as distinct and coeternal persons, are of one indivisible divine essence. Supporting the doctrine of the Trinity is known as Trinitarianism.

triadic. In logic, mathematics, and semiotics, a triadic relation (or a ternary relation) is an important special case of a polyadic or finitary relation in which the number of places in the relation is three. One also sees the adjectives "3-adic," "3-ary," "3-dim," or "3-place" to describe their relations.

Mathematics is positively rife with examples of 3-adic relations, and a sign relation, the archidea of the whole field of semiotics, is a special case of a 3-adic relation.

willpower. This is your inner strength, which is all about self-control and determination. You cannot develop willpower, but you can try to manifest it. Willpower exists in its perfection.

About the Authors

Ralph H. Boyce and **Pastor Gloria Taylor-Boyce** are lovers of people. They are adult educators, published authors, lifestyle coaches, motivational speakers, communication specialists, and master and licensed trainers of Neuro-Linguistic Programming (NLP). Their vision is to enrich people's lives by using their pastoral anointing and NLP training to demonstrate to partners how to build a more prosperous future and be all they can perceive themselves to be.

Pastor Ralph H. Boyce is the senior pastor of Zoe Ministries International –Canada, where he and his wife, Pastor Gloria Taylor-Boyce, an award-winning, best-selling author, team up to teach many programs.

Pastor Gloria Taylor-Boyce. The headline of a recent news release read, "Business Expert Gloria Taylor-Boyce Hits Amazon Best-Seller List." It continues on to say: "Author and Pastor Gloria Taylor-Boyce recently hit five separate Amazon.com best-seller lists with her book *Cracking the Success Code*. The book was released by Celebrity Press, a leading business book publisher."

Author and pastor Gloria Taylor-Boyce, an expert in team building and leadership skills, has joined with a select group of the world's leading business experts and with best-selling author and speaker Brian Tracy to coauthor the book titled *Cracking the Success Code: The World's Leading Experts Reveal Their Top Secrets to Help You Crack the Code for Optimum Health, Wealth, and Success.* This book won her a Quilly Award.

Pastor Gloria Taylor-Boyce is the author of the books *Why Are You Here?*, *Watts in Your Hands*, *Cracking the Success Code*, *Discerning Your True Spiritual Calling*, and now *You Cannot Fail!*

Pastor Gloria also conducts an online coaching club for budding authors called The Writers' Club.

As members of the Zoeland Writers' Club, you will follow a proven writing system developed by Pastor Gloria Taylor-Boyce. You will also write and publish your books. Take charge of your future! http://www.thenewwritersclub.com/

Pastor Ralph H. Boyce and Pastor Gloria Taylor-Boyce conduct NLP classes at the Zoeland Institute of NLP (www.nlpmindchange.com) They are also pastors of the church:

Zoe Ministries International, Canada
Marriott Fairfield Inn & Suites Brampton
150 Westcreek Blvd.
Brampton, Ontario L6T 5V7
** Bramalea Room **

www.zoecanada.org or
1-905-794-7358
1-800-441-0239, ext. 2

CPSIA information can be obtained at www.ICGtesting.com
Printed in the USA
LVOW10s1947121114

413338LV00035B/2360/P